"*The Whole Life* should be require has the potential to make or breal rarely addressed in formal training of God's grace for sinners, the tool of thriving in ministry."

Dan Passerelli, President, Metro Baltimore Seminary

"We could all use some help in our devotions. What sets this book apart is its holistic approach to the care of one's own soul. While underscoring God's supremacy in our lives, we are also encouraged in this weekly format to consider the emotional, relational, and embodied aspects of our lives that are often overlooked. This book would also make a great resource for counselees!"

Eric L. Johnson, Professor of Christian Psychology, Gideon Institute of Christian Psychology & Counseling, Houston Baptist University

"Those who devote their lives to the care of others often fail to properly care for themselves. In their timely and needed book, Eliza and Esther offer Scripture-saturated, practical wisdom for self-care. They carefully recast our understanding of self-care as a biblically rooted habit and offer guidance on how to make self-care a life-giving practice. This book contains fifty-two weeks of soul-feeding content and is a gift to the care of God's children!"

Andrew Dealy, Director of Soul Care and Executive Director, The Austin Stone Counseling Center, The Austin Stone Community Church

"When we hear about self-care, our first reaction is often to ask, 'Should we really care for ourselves? Shouldn't our focus be exclusively on sacrificial care for others?' I appreciate Eliza Huie and Esther Smith's biblically-based definition of self-care: 'the practice of drawing on divinely-given resources to steward our whole lives for personal enrichment, the good of others, and the glory of God.' In *The Whole Life*, they comprehensively and compassionately help readers to steward their lives so that they can live a lifetime of ministry to others to the glory of God."

Bob Kellemen, Academic Dean, Dean of Students, and Professor of Biblical Counseling, Faith Bible Seminary, Lafayette, Indiana

"Stewardship is a word in Scripture that often is only associated with money. But the fact is, stewardship is about everything God has given us, including our body and soul. Eliza and Esther wisely call us to pay attention to ways we must steward these gifts."

Timothy S. Lane, President, Institute for Pastoral Care and Tim Lane & Associates; author of *Unstuck: A Nine-Step Journey to Change that Lasts*; coauthor of *Relationships: A Mess Worth Making* and *How People Change*

"*The Whole Life* provides a grace-filled and compelling vision for Christian self-care. All of us who struggle to live as holistic disciples should take this fifty-two-week journey toward caring for our bodies and souls in a gospel-saturated way. The exercises are simple and thought-provoking, and every week serves as a reminder of the beauty of honoring and enjoying God in every area of life."

Beth M. Broom, LPC Supervisor and Care Minister, The Village Church, Denton

"This book is thoughtfully written, practically presented, theologically-rich, hope-filled, and robustly relevant. As a pastor, professor, counselor, and business owner, my heart resonated with all of it. The weekly format drew me in and kept me focused on first things being first, while creating such an engaging format for my already busy yet productive life. I'd highly recommend pastors, professors, ministry leaders, business owners, and volunteers to read it."

Dwayne R. Bond, Lead Pastor, Wellspring Church; owner of Proximus Group, LLC

"Practical, biblical, and insightful, *The Whole Life* is a needed reminder for those of us who struggle with self-care that the Lord calls us to steward our lives with intentionality, wisdom, and a sensitivity to the Spirit's leading. If you feel overworked, stressed, and can't figure out what to do about it, this book is for you!"

Vaneetha Rendall Risner, Author of *Walking Through Fire: A Memoir of Loss and Redemption*

"When you think of self-care, do you immediately feel guilty for even thinking about it? *The Whole Life* not only shows the necessity of self-care, but also the utter biblical grounding for this idea of stewarding all of your life as a gift from God to be used in service to love others. Esther and Eliza do a remarkable job in giving you a place to practice self-care in a biblically healthy way. I would recommend this to every counselor, pastor, and people-helper."

Cache Barnes, Executive Director, Redemption: Twin Cities

"The term *self-care* has certainly become an elusive buzzword in today's society. It's something I prescribe for others while often failing to consistently engage in myself. In *The Whole Life*, Eliza and Esther journey with you for a year and provide weekly, practical steps to implement this practice. They use a biblical approach to remind you that caring for the spirit, soul, and body is not selfish, but simply stewardship."

Renee Davis, Clinical Psychologist

"God has entrusted us all to be good stewards of our bodies, emotions, and relationships. In *The Whole Life*, Eliza Huie and Esther Smith lay out a foundation for the kind of biblical self-care that is necessary to fuel a life lived wholly for the glory of God. I invite everyone experiencing exhaustion or burnout to pick up this book and put its contents into practice!"

Walter Shaw, Blogger at *WTSreads*

THE WHOLE LIFE
52 WEEKS OF
BIBLICAL SELF-CARE

Eliza Huie and Esther Smith

New
Growth
Press

newgrowthpress.com

New Growth Press, Greensboro, NC 27404
newgrowthpress.com

Cover Design: Faceout Books, faceoutstudio.com
Interior Design and Typesetting: Gretchen Logterman

ISBN: 978-1-64507-135-8 (Print)
ISBN: 978-1-64507-136-5 (eBook)

Library of Congress Cataloging-in-Publication Data
Names: Huie, Eliza, author. | Smith, Esther (Biblical Counselor), author.
Title: The whole life : 52 weeks of biblical self-care / Eliza Huie and
    Esther Smith.
Description: Greensboro, NC : New Growth Press, [2021] | Includes
    bibliographical references. | Summary: "Counselors Eliza Huie and Esther
    Smith give Christians a framework for biblical self-care that will help
    them live for Christ by stewarding the spiritual, emotional, and
    physical aspects of life"-- Provided by publisher.
Identifiers: LCCN 2021008599 (print) | LCCN 2021008600 (ebook) | ISBN
    9781645071358 (trade paperback) | ISBN 9781645071365 (ebook)
Subjects: LCSH: Christian life.--Miscellanea.
Classification: LCC BV4501.3 .H843 2021 (print) | LCC BV4501.3 (ebook) |
    DDC 248.4--dc23
LC record available at https://lccn.loc.gov/2021008599
LC ebook record available at https://lccn.loc.gov/2021008600

Printed in the United States of America

28 27 26 25 24 23 22 21   1 2 3 4 5

CONTENTS

Section 4: Community Life

Section 5: Work Life

Section 6: A Restful Life

INTRODUCTION

Is your life overscheduled? Is your health telling you to take a break? Are you stressed or exhausted but feel guilty slowing down? Is the idea of caring for yourself a foreign concept? Or maybe the idea of setting aside time for yourself makes you feel vaguely guilty. Your commitment to follow Christ encourages you to give selflessly, but perhaps you are starting to wonder if you have sacrificed to your own demise. If any of this sounds like we have somehow read your mail or have been spying on your world, we invite you to join us on this journey of caring for yourself.

This book is for Christians who are committed to loving God and loving others; it is for believers who pour their lives out in sacrificial service. You might be a parent or caretaker serving those within your own household. You may spend your workdays contributing to the good and well-being of others as a medical professional, first responder, social worker, teacher, business owner, or executive. Perhaps you are a pastor, counselor, Bible study leader, or church volunteer who selflessly gives of your time and energy. No matter your particular role, you pour yourself out until you have almost nothing left.

We've been there too. Our stories below reveal how important self-care is in stewarding our whole life for the good of others and the glory of God.

ELIZA'S STORY

There are many ways to describe me. Personality tests label me as the entrepreneur, an extrovert, the giver, a Myers-Briggs type ENFJ, or Enneagram type Three. I've been described as driven. I naturally wake up early and hit the day running. I love creating new ventures and improving on others. I love saying yes and hate saying no to opportunity. And "wait" certainly is a four-letter word.

Slowing down is not easy for me. Because of this, I can neglect the good things God has given me that bring refreshment and replenishment. Things like rest, silence, being creative, enjoying nature, engaging with friends, pausing to be present, and other things that get lost in the hurry of life. A few years ago, the reality of this pace hit me hard, and I started constantly feeling overwhelmed. The stress manifested itself in ways I felt in my entire body.

I could not ignore the physical realities and the decline in my health. I also was dealing with the spiritual and emotional impact the pace and demands were having on me. I came to realize I could not keep up by just working harder. Something had to change.

God, in his kindness, graciously met me in that season and taught me important lessons I will never forget. In the pages of this book, I will share some of these lessons that yielded valuable life changes. I am still a doer and a goer, but with God's help, I do and go with a better understanding of balance and God's grace. However, I easily drift. The pull is strong to return to a frenetic pace of life.

Someone once told me, "Write the book you want to read." For me, this project goes beyond that advice. This is the book I *need* to read! So, while I write this book for you, I need this book as well. I need the reminders. I need the direction. I need the rhythms. It is a continual call back to the care I so easily neglect. This book honors our humanity, our limits, and the God who created them. I trust it will serve you as we journey together into what it means to care for the person who is in your life every moment of every day—you.

ESTHER'S STORY

Over ten years ago, my life was interrupted by chronic pain and autoimmune illness. It soon became apparent that I would need to make major life adjustments to manage my symptoms. After years of searching for answers, I was diagnosed with lupus, and since then, I have found it necessary to slow down and revolve much of my daily life around self-care.

In general, I am good at self-care. Even as I write that sentence, I'm tempted to wonder if I am fooling myself. Isn't being "good at self-care" just code for being lazy or selfish? On occasion, doubts like these still linger in the back of my mind, but nowadays, these doubts happen much less often.

Self-care doesn't feel like a choice for me. It's more of a life necessity. This has led me to spend a lot of time considering what God says about this topic, and over the years, I have found a great deal of freedom to prioritize caring for my body and my soul. I prioritize rest, say no to things I want to do, plan my schedule around medical appointments, and simplify daily tasks when they start to feel detrimental to my body. I am still figuring out the balance between living my life and succumbing to the rest my body needs. What I do know for sure is that without a focus on self-care, my body would deteriorate, and I would struggle to continue meeting my responsibilities each day.

On those days when I would rather push through to the detriment of my health, I need to be reminded that taking care of myself is good and honors God. I also need to be reminded that self-care isn't about me. As you will soon read in the coming pages, self-care is about maximizing the ways God can work through me—and you—for other people, and ultimately, his glory.

YOUR STORY

We are different people with different stories, but we have each discovered a need for self-care that is one and the same. You also have a unique story, and we think you will discover your need is similar to ours. We all need self-care.

Over the next year, you will consider truths from Scripture that relate to stewarding your resources in six areas: your spiritual life, your physical life, your purposeful approach to life, your community life, your work life, and your life of rest. Each week includes a thoughtful entry on a self-care topic. Following each entry, you will find a **Gospel Spotlight** intended to point you to Jesus. An **Action and Application** section will help you implement practical self-care strategies for the good of your spiritual, emotional, physical, and relational well-being. You will also find a **Guided Journaling** section that will enable you to engage the content more personally. We encourage you to have a designated place such as a journal or note in your phone for writing out your thoughts and personal applications.

While this book is designed to be worked through on your own, it is also incredibly valuable to read with others. Consider asking someone to join you on this journey. Who in your life might benefit from observing a year of whole-life stewardship? For example, could you gather a group of friends together for mutual accountability? Perhaps your ministry team, fellow classmates, or family members would benefit from this discussion as well. Practicing self-care in community provides helpful support as you engage challenging topics and consider difficult changes.

Our hope is that this book becomes a gift to you and expands your understanding of how truly valuable self-care is to yourself and others. At one point when we attended the same church, the founding pastor, Michael Crawford, was known to say these words: "We take care of ourselves so we can love well and live well." He is right. As you use this book and focus on stewarding your whole life, we pray it inspires a lifelong commitment to self-care that increases your capacity to love others. We pray it points you back to your Creator, who gives good gifts to steward for his glory.

SECTION 1
SPIRITUAL LIFE

WEEK 1
WHAT IS BIBLICAL SELF-CARE?

Take care of your body as if you were going to live forever; and
take care of your soul as if you were going to die tomorrow.

Augustine

Embracing the idea of self-care can feel uncomfortable. The
word isn't found in Scripture, and some Christians may wonder
if self-care is contrary to a sacrificial life. Doesn't the Bible call us
to put the care of others first? Won't attending to self-care lead
to selfishness? These common questions and concerns often arise
when we don't consider a biblical understanding of the principles behind self-care.

Self-care is an extrabiblical word that contains essential biblical truth. We define biblical self-care as the practice of drawing
on divinely given resources to steward our whole lives for personal enrichment, the good of others, and the glory of God. We
don't practice self-care because it's trendy. We practice self-care
because it's a biblical concept. We embrace self-care as a way to
steward our souls, minds, bodies, and relationships. This whole-
life stewardship is an act of obedience to God's call to love others
as we love ourselves. The following concepts explain biblical self-
care as seen in Scripture.

Biblical self-care is stewardship. We are called to steward everything God gives us. A steward manages and cares for resources.
This stewardship principle goes beyond financial and material

resources. We are to be good stewards of God's varied graces, including ourselves (Luke 12:48; 2 Corinthians 9:6–15; 1 Peter 4:10). God gave us bodies that need care. He gave us souls that need attention. Scripture affirms the reality of human needs and does not discourage meeting those needs. Numerous places in the Bible describe, even encourage, paying appropriate attention to caring for ourselves (1 Kings 19:1–8; Matthew 15:32; Mark 6:31–32; Acts 20:28; Ephesians 5:29).

Biblical self-care is modeled by Jesus. Jesus is God in human flesh. In Scripture we see him give attention to his human needs. When he was hungry, he ate. When he was tired, he rested. When he needed time alone with the Father, he made this a priority. As the perfect man, his whole life was perfectly balanced. Not only did he model stewardship of his body, mind, soul, and relationships, he also encouraged others to do the same (Mark 1:35; 11:12; 12:31; John 4:6).

Biblical self-care is rooted in creation. We see this most clearly in the institution of the Sabbath in Genesis 2:1–3. Rest is part of our original created design and a key component of biblical self-care. From the beginning of time, God's divine intention was that we stop and pause from the demands of life and work. While rest refreshes our bodies, minds, souls, and relationships, it's also a proclamation of trust. We rest as an act of trust-filled worship, declaring God as our creator and sustainer. God intended these pauses to reaffirm in our hearts that he will supply all that we need as we obey the command to rest (Exodus 20:8–11; Philippians 4:19).

Biblical self-care is a blessing to others. Scripture teaches that we are to love one another (Romans 12:10) and do good to everyone (Galatians 6:10). As we give Christlike attention to our own needs, we are equipped to show Christlike love for others in need. God enriches us in every way so we can be generous in every way (2 Corinthians 9:11). Wisely caring for ourselves according to God's Word enables us to effectively pour ourselves into the lives of others.

Biblical self-care is tied to the gospel. As we have just seen, self-care is important because it helps us to love others well. Our love for others is motivated by the gospel. We love others because Jesus first loved us (1 John 4:7–11). The most important way we love others is by sharing with them the good news of what Jesus has done. Our ability to do this is tied to how well we care for ourselves. We fulfill the Great Commission in our bodies, with our minds, through our relationships, and as an outpouring of what Jesus has done for our own souls (Matthew 28:18-20; 2 Corinthians 5:18–21).

These concepts support self-care as an important priority for Christians. Sadly, believers are often left feeling guilty or ashamed for embracing practices of self-care. Taking time away for refreshment or spending money for things that encourage physical or emotional wellness are often seen as frivolous or selfish. Taking needed breaks from the demands of life to take a nap, read a good book, or take a walk are met with disapproval when progress is halted. In certain seasons of life, it may be more difficult to figure out how to practice self-care in a way that is biblical. We will address this more in Week 44 and Week 51. However, regardless of circumstances, believers should not be shamed when attending to their needs but rather encouraged to care for themselves.

Have these biblical truths challenged your perspective? This week you will assess your personal views on self-care and consider how God might be inviting you to change your approach to caring for yourself. To get the most out of the action and application sections we encourage you to engage each question prayerfully and attentively.

GOSPEL SPOTLIGHT

As important as self-care may be, it's not our most pressing need. What we need most is Jesus. In him we lack nothing (Psalm 23:1). He is the source of our physical, spiritual, emotional, and relational health. We have nothing to offer others that we have not received from him (John 15:1–27).

ACTION AND APPLICATION

Spiritual: What message have you received from Christian teachers or other believers about self-care? How has that impacted your understanding of God's view of caring for yourself?

Emotional: What emotions come up when you think about practicing self-care? How do those emotions align with the concepts of biblical self-care stated above?

Physical: Scripture teaches that our bodies are temples of the Holy Spirit (1 Corinthians 6:19). Our bodies are to be used to bring God glory. How well do you take care of your body?

Relational: Have you experienced pushback in your relationships when you take time to care for yourself? Think about how you can address this tension biblically. Use the Scriptures from this week's reading to help you.

GUIDED JOURNALING

How well are you caring for yourself? On a scale of one to ten, give yourself a rating on how you are doing. One equals little to no self-care. Ten equals self-care is a regular part of your routine. Jot down your number. As you think about your rating, what changes do you feel compelled to make?

WEEK 2
TIME OUT WITH GOD

And rising very early in the morning, while it was still dark, he
departed and went out to a desolate place, and there he prayed.

Mark 1:35

As a counselor, one of the most unique opportunities to care for
people took me (Eliza) to Fujinomiya, Japan. This small town
sits at the base of Mount Fuji. It wasn't the drastically different
culture and language that made this experience so unique. It was
the fact that I was asked to counsel in a way I had never done
before. In an effort to care for the missionaries serving in Japan,
I was part of a small team providing counseling at a major mis-
sions conference. We had three days to offer one or two counseling sessions to the five hundred missionaries in attendance.
Think speed dating meets counseling and you have a pretty good
picture of what we were doing.

Our short trip consisted of early-morning starts and late-
night endings. Considering Japan is thirteen time zones ahead
of the United States, we were doing all of this in what our bodies
thought was the middle of the night. By the time we got back to
our rooms each night there wasn't much more we wanted to do
than lie on the floor (quite literally in Japan) and sleep.

Before this trip, the Lord taught me something I would des-
perately need to apply during this time of jam-packed serving. The
lesson came from the first chapter of Mark. It was the beginning

of Jesus's ministry on earth. He had become known for his authority over demons and his power to heal, and people were flocking to him en masse. Mark's description says, "the whole city was gathered together at the door" of the house where he was staying (Mark 1:33). They wanted his care. They needed his care.

The next day people were still coming. They were looking for the man who had the power to help and heal them. But Jesus was nowhere to be found. His disciples looked all over for him. The need was great. The people were pressing. Where was Jesus? We learn from Mark 1:35 that Jesus had gotten up very early in the morning to be alone and pray. In this act, Jesus models one of the most powerful principles of self-care. Pressing needs do not negate the importance of being alone in prayer to meet with God.

Jesus showed us that staying connected to the Father is vital no matter how demanding our lives may be. Time out with God fueled his ability to move forward and accomplish the mission God had ordained for him. He continued to engage fully in ministry but only after spending time alone with God.

At the base of Mount Fuji, Jesus's example became real for me. I woke up very early every morning. I wish I could say it was something more spiritual, but honestly, the jet lag woke me up before the sun each day. In these early morning hours before anyone else was awake and asking for my help, the first thing that came to my mind was Mark 1:35. I took very early morning walks to pray and be alone with the Father. I listened to God through his Word. Those times of prayer and meditation sustained me in a tremendously demanding time of ministry.

Life gets demanding. You may find yourself overwhelmed with juggling work, home, and serving. It may seem like there just isn't enough of you to go around. In times like these, we must commit all the more to taking time out to be alone with God. It may not be early in the morning. It could be late at night or in the middle of the day. The key is that we prioritize time alone with God to spiritually care for ourselves in the midst of caring for others. We cannot properly pour out to others if we are empty.

GOSPEL SPOTLIGHT

When Jesus took time to be with the Father this was much more than him setting a good example for us. It also points to the reality of what the cross accomplished for every believer. Through Jesus, we have open access to the Father twenty-four hours a day, seven days a week.

ACTION AND APPLICATION

Spiritual: When your days are busy with serving or caring for others, do the demands of life fill all the spaces of your day? This week set aside a specific time to meet with God alone.

Emotional: Do emotional struggles increase when you don't prioritize time alone with God? What emotional cues could suggest you need to reprioritize time alone with God?

Physical: When demands are high it's easy to get distracted in our efforts to pray and read the Bible. Following the example of Jesus can help. This week try changing your physical location when you pray. Find an outside space or other place where you can be alone with God.

Relational: It's easy to forget that the context of our engagement with God is a relationship, and relationships require investment. Assess your relationship with God. What areas do you need to strengthen?

GUIDED JOURNALING

Read Acts 17:24–28 and use the passage to orient your heart. Journal specific ways you can prioritize time with God this week.

WEEK 3
HEALING POWER OF THE WORD

The Word is living and active. It will conform you by
dividing you. And in the dividing, miracle of miracles, it
will render you whole.

Jen Wilkin

Have you ever been the creator of your own demise? We sure
have. If you are like us, you can become overcommitted, overwhelmed, and overworked because of a lack of wisdom or
healthy boundaries. What first seemed like a God-ordained opportunity to serve or a call to minister and care for someone is
now a daunting burden. Or maybe you say yes too often to the
requests from your job or family, leaving you exhausted or extended beyond your capacity.

Sometimes the opposite is true. It isn't that we took on too
much, but that we avoided too much. We neglected a nagging
and difficult task or ignored the need to chip away at a responsibility, and now we are far behind. We don't need other people to
create trouble for us. We create plenty on our own.

Psalm 107 is a reminder that we are not the first people who
have been known to make life complicated for ourselves. God's
people had the same experience in Psalm 107:17–20. This passage exemplifies how God meets us in our trouble with healing,
even if we have brought on our own distress: "Some were fools
through their sinful ways, and because of their inequities suffered

affliction; they loathed any kind of food, and they drew near to the gates of death. Then they cried to the LORD in their trouble, and he delivered them from their distress. He sent out his word and healed them, and delivered them from their destruction."

The psalm describes people so upset by their circumstances that they can't even eat. What is worse is that they caused this situation because of their unwise and sinful choices. Notice what helps them in this situation. They cry to God for help, and he heals and rescues them by sending out his Word. What we need in moments of distress is to hear from God. We need his Word.

God's Word heals as it changes our hearts (Hebrews 4:12). His Word gives needed direction when the path ahead is unclear (Psalm 119:105). His Word orients our hearts to set better priorities (Matthew 6:33). Most importantly, God's Word has the power to sanctify us (John 17:17). That is healing. That is rescue.

As our hearts are changed by God's Word, we have a new perspective and direction. This shows us how important it is to be listening to God through his Word. We need to treasure God's Word in our hearts to keep us from making sinful decisions that leave us feeling overwhelmed and exhausted (Psalm 119:11). When we find ourselves in distress, we can cry out to the Lord and seek him in his Word. There we will find healing, help, and renewal.

GOSPEL SPOTLIGHT

Jesus is called the Word in John 1:14. He came to earth and dwelt among us. Let this truth now point you to the ultimate healing we have in the Word who became flesh.

ACTION AND APPLICATION

Spiritual: When life is full of trouble do you turn toward or away from God's Word? What is one change you can make this week to engage God's Word regularly?

Emotional: What would it look like to cry out to the Lord? Through prayer, try bringing honest, emotional concerns to him today.

Physical: In Psalm 107 people experienced a physical response in their distress; they didn't want to eat, and they felt like they were near to death. How have you experienced physical responses to distress? Use the Body Scan Activity in the appendix and identify where distress is manifesting in your body.

Relational: How is God bringing healing into your life through his Word? Share your thoughts with one trusted person this week. To help you follow though, write the person's name here.

GUIDED JOURNALING

As you reflect on the questions above, use your journal to finish this prayer: God, your Word brings healing as it works in my heart. Remind me of your Truth that heals. I need healing in . . .

I need your help with . . .

WEEK 4
PRACTICING BIBLICAL MEDITATION

Today I seek you, O God. Please fill me with the capacity to
keep my mind focused during the seeking moments.

Barbara L. Peacock

What comes to mind when you think about meditation? Perhaps
your mind immediately fills with concerns of Buddhism or New
Age practices. You might associate meditation with seeking to
achieve self-actualization instead of focusing on Christ. Maybe
you are open to the practice but have been taught to proceed with
caution. You know Scripture talks about it, but you also see a fine
line between meditation that's biblical and meditation that's not.

Biblical meditation focuses on truths from God's Word,
seeking to understand how they apply to our lives. Some people
are so wary of using meditation in wrong ways that they ignore
this valuable and biblical practice. In reality, we all meditate.
When life becomes busy and difficult, we ruminate over our
worries and concerns. When life doesn't pan out the way we
want it to, we dream or fantasize about the way life "should" be.
Meditation happens any time we fixate our mind on a thought
and stay there. What are *you* meditating on today?

Scripture recognizes our tendency to meditate on our anx-
ieties (Philippians 4:5) and invites us to instead deeply reflect
on things that are true (Philippians 4:8). Instead of ruminating
on problems, insecurities, or fears, Scripture encourages us to

meditate on God's law (Psalm 1:2), God's works (Psalm 143:5), and God's promises (Psalm 119:148). Meditation is an opportunity to remind ourselves of essential truths we easily forget but need each and every day.

I (Esther) practice meditation by drawing from my daily Bible reading. As I read, I pick a short phrase that I want to focus on throughout the day. It could be a phrase that sticks out to me, or a concept that's especially relevant to me that day. I then use meditation as a bridge between reading Scripture and praying. I close my eyes and take a few moments to fixate my mind on a short truth, considering how God might be speaking to me and how he might want me to live out his Word that day.

Fixing our thoughts on the promises of Scripture affects our minds, bodies, and souls. Meditation can reduce the number, speed, and intensity of our thoughts. It reduces tension in our bodies, especially when paired with the deep breathing exercise found in the appendix. On a spiritual level, meditating on the truth of Scripture connects us with God and often helps his promises to stick with us throughout the day.

Try practicing meditation right now. Think of a short passage of Scripture. You might pick a favorite passage, or if you aren't sure where to start, read through Psalm 23 slowly and pick a phrase that sticks out to you. Find a quiet place to be alone. Then sit or lie down in a comfortable position. Set a timer for two to five minutes and close your eyes. Take a few deep breaths and allow your mind to dwell on the phrase you have chosen. Remember that God is present with you. What might God be saying to you through this Scripture? How does this Scripture encourage or convict you? How might God be asking you to live out this verse today? As you reflect, what are you compelled to pray?

As you dwell on the verse, don't be concerned if your mind becomes distracted and drifts to worries or tasks of the day. Simply notice when this happens and gently bring your thoughts back to the verse until the timer goes off. Open your eyes and consider for a moment how you feel and how God met you during your time of reflection.

GOSPEL SPOTLIGHT

One day this week, meditate on a verse that helps you recall the heart of the gospel. For example, "There is therefore now no condemnation for those who are in Christ Jesus" (Romans 8:1); or "Come to me, all who labor and are heavy laden, and I will give you rest" (Matthew 11:28).

ACTION AND APPLICATION

Spiritual: Ask God to help you identify several Scriptures or general truths you most need to remember in your current season of life. Write them down, memorize them, and use meditation to draw on these verses when you need them.

Emotional: How did meditating today influence your emotional state? Did you notice any difference between how you felt before and after meditating?

Physical: Experiment with different physical postures while you meditate: lying down, kneeling, sitting, et cetera. Notice how posture affects your ability to concentrate.

Relational: If you have concerns about practicing meditation, talk to someone about it. What are your specific concerns? Do you have any lingering questions that a Christian mentor or friend might be able to answer?

GUIDED JOURNALING

How can you incorporate meditation into your life? Some people find it helpful to schedule time for meditation in their morning or evening routine. Others use it as they drive to work, take a shower, or during some other fixed daily marker. Still others choose to use meditation to help them sleep or in moments of distress. What might work for you and your schedule? In your journal, write about one way you will include biblical meditation into your week.

WEEK 5
SEEK HIS STRENGTH CONTINUALLY

> You may forget that you are at every moment totally
> dependent on God.
>
> *C. S. Lewis*

My (Esther's) counseling supervisor often reminds our staff of the importance of bringing God into our counseling relationships.[1] As we sit across from people and listen to their complex stories, there are times when their struggles feel beyond us. We don't have all the answers to their questions. We aren't quite sure all the best ways to help. On the outside we look calm, but on the inside, our minds wonder, *What should I say next?*

We are most prone to mistakes in moments like this when we try to proceed alone and forget that God is in the counseling room with us. We can always ask him for help. When we stop to pray in moments of uncertainty, God often makes it clear when we should stay silent, or he gives us words we couldn't have come up with on our own.

This reminder to seek God's strength in the middle of my counseling sessions has helped me grow as a counselor. It has also been an invaluable reminder in my day-to-day life. Every day we face a myriad of struggles and decisions, and we often forget to bring God into the picture. Even when we start the day strong, going to God and reading his Word in the morning, it's surprising how often we forget about him as soon as we close our Bibles. This has consequences. It often leads to poor decisions, despairing emotions, regrettable interactions, and living for ourselves.

Psalm 105:4 reminds us to "Seek the Lord and his strength; seek his presence continually!" This is practical advice that leads to a practical response. In difficult daily conversations, we can practice pausing and ask God for wisdom to know what to say. In times of suffering, remembering God helps us believe there is purpose in what we are going through. As we face challenging decisions, this is an opportunity to seek God and align our desires with his.

As you go through this week, build an awareness of which sins and sufferings tend to intensify for you when you forget about God. Are certain sins easier for you to fall into when you live outside an awareness of his presence? Does irritability and annoyance with people increase when you neglect intentionally connecting with God before starting your day? Do you tend to make regrettable decisions when you don't go to God for guidance? What areas of suffering, if any, feel more difficult when you forget God is with you and for you?

Seeking God's presence can be a form of self-care that ultimately benefits everyone we encounter. As we repeatedly go to God, he infuses us with strength, wisdom, and patience. This not only helps us better tackle the challenges of our day, it also equips us to love other people well.

GOSPEL SPOTLIGHT

We can enter God's presence with confidence, full assurance of faith, and a clear conscience because of Christ's sacrifice (Hebrews 10:19–22). He is why we have direct access to God and his strength at all times.

ACTION AND APPLICATION

Spiritual: What sins and struggles tend to intensify for you when you forget about God? Pay close attention this week and write out a list.

Emotional: What is your most difficult emotional struggle right now? Come up with a one-sentence prayer you can use throughout the day to ask God for help and strength in that area.

Physical: Identify a physical reminder that can help you remember to seek God's presence continually. For example, write out a reminder on a note card, set an alarm on your phone, or use a specific room in your house as a cue every time you enter it.

Relational: Irritability, selfishness, and apathy toward other people's problems tend to increase when we aren't connected with God. How are your relationships impacted when you forget to seek God's strength?

GUIDED JOURNALING

Take some time to connect with God right now. Journal out a prayer to him. Ask for strength. Ask him to continually remind you throughout the day that he's an ever-present help in times of stress and trouble.

WEEK 6
YOU CAN HAVE JESUS AND A COUNSELOR TOO

> Here is the sweet paradox in how God works. He blesses those
> who admit that they need help.
>
> *David Powlison*

"Is there a back door?" The man in his mid-thirties had called
to inquire about setting up an initial counseling appointment
to discuss his unrelenting feelings of depression. He asked great
questions and was relieved to hear of the care he could receive
from a counselor. Once he confirmed his appointment, he
sheepishly asked, "Is there a back door?"

I (Eliza) stumbled to think how his question connected to
the rest of our conversation. Why does he care about the back
door? He went on to explain that he felt guilty about seeing a
counselor. Shouldn't his faith be enough? It was a daunting question to which he did not have an answer. He asked about the
back door as a way to circumvent any possibility of being seen
going into a counseling center and therefore avoid any possible
unwanted guilt and judgment.

Counseling is a means of getting focused care and input regarding your struggles and sufferings. It can be a healthy part of
an overall journey toward wholeness. But that may not be how
you have been taught to view counseling. You may resonate more

with the man in the story above. You might have learned directly or indirectly that all that you will ever need is found in Jesus alone. Don't verses like Psalm 62:2 affirm that "He alone is my rock and my salvation"? How should this man, and how might you, make sense of this tension when considering seeing a counselor?

Believing in Jesus does not eliminate a need for outside help. If that were true, you should stop seeing the dentist, the doctor, or even the mechanic for that matter. All you need is to pray and wait for the Lord's provision. But what happens when you pray, have faith, and believe, but things don't get better? Maybe they even get worse. What do you do? Where can you go?

The stigma sometimes attached to counseling is not totally unfounded. After all, Freud, the father of psychology, was critical of religion and was obsessed with a hypersexualized view of people's struggles. Many secular models of psychology emphasize a fixation on self that is idolatrous. There's reason to raise an eyebrow of concern.

Before you surrender counseling over to the secular world, consider that the Bible spoke of counseling and counselors long before Freud and his contemporaries. Numerous places in Proverbs speak of the wisdom of counsel (Proverbs 12:15; 13:10; 15:22). An entire chapter in 1 Chronicles has a list of people who served the king. This list specifically included counselors (1 Chronicles 27:32–33). Jesus himself was called the Wonderful Counselor (Isaiah 9:6).

Faith in Jesus and counseling are not opposed to each other, especially if a biblical counselor connects the truths of the Scripture to your life. You don't have to choose between Jesus and counseling. Counseling that aligns with the message of the Bible is not a deviation from your faith in Jesus. Instead it can help you see how to daily depend on the work of Jesus to sanctify you and make you more like him. Often it is evidence of a humble spirit that acknowledges, "I need help."

GOSPEL SPOTLIGHT

God's provision of care includes giving us his people (Philemon 1:7). God uses his people as a means to meet Jesus. It's not just that you can have Jesus *and* counseling. When your care comes from one of God's children, you are often brought to a place to see Jesus *in* counseling.

ACTION AND APPLICATION

Spiritual: Consider what Proverbs 11:14; 12:15; and 15:22 say about counseling. Ask God to reveal any shame you have related to the possibility of pursuing the help of a counselor.

Emotional: Are you wrestling with anything right now that you cannot solve on your own? How is that impacting your emotional health? Be intentional this week to seek out counsel from a trusted friend, pastor, or biblical counselor.

Physical: Bottling up stress can lead to physical symptoms. Counselors help people manage stress more effectively. List one or two stressful situations you are currently dealing with that might be causing physical issues. Consider talking to a counselor about what you write down.

Relational: Are any of your relationships currently impacted by your own personal need for counseling? If so, take a step of humility and seek counsel today.

GUIDED JOURNALING

Take time to jot down what you might want to talk to a counselor about. If you choose to make an appointment, bring this journal entry with you to your first session.

WEEK 7
SPIRITUAL DISCIPLINES
IN DRY SEASONS

The Lord has promised good to me. His Word, my hope secures.

John Newton

We love the practicality of spiritual disciplines. Through spiritual disciplines, God graciously gives us specific ways we can draw near to him to be transformed by him. Although we will focus on just two spiritual disciplines this week—reading the Word and prayer—the general principles we discuss can also be applied to other disciplines such as fasting, meditation, solitude, confession, and worship.

In various seasons of life, God often gives us an urge to dig deep and draw closer to him. This urge sometimes comes out of suffering. Other times, it arises seemingly out of nowhere. No matter the reason, these times often lead to a flurry of growth and connection with God. Then, all too often, as quickly as they come, these mountaintop moments seem to disappear.

For each season of longing for the Word, another season of unexplained apathy can follow. Seasons when reading Scripture feels hard. Times when prayer feels impossible. Too many mornings in life, we look at our Bibles and wonder why we have no desire to pick up God's Word. Guilt quickly arises. Shame creeps to the surface. Questions soon follow. *What is wrong with me? Why can't I get it together?*

God invites us on a lifelong journey of drawing closer to him and becoming more like him. Ideally, we would always "long for the pure milk of the word" (1 Peter 2:2 NASB). Our souls would always thirst for God (Psalm 42:2). What should we do when these longings disappear?

All Christians experience normal variations in their desire for God. Legitimate struggles and distractions come between us and our Bibles. Prayer can be difficult for many reasons. Some people find that physical and emotional struggles impair their concentration. For others, caring for small children or managing a busy work schedule leaves little time for anything else. The presence of suffering, sin, or doubt can complicate our relationship with God and reduce our desire to seek him. Other times it's unclear why spiritual disciplines are difficult. Sometimes they just are. This is one of the reasons we call them disciplines. They are purposeful habits we build into our lives so we can return to them continually in both dry and abundant seasons.

In addition to building habits into our lives, a change in perspective can help us press on. Throughout Scripture, God's Word is compared to food. Deuteronomy 8:3 says, "man does not live by bread alone, but man lives by every word that comes from the mouth of the LORD." Scripture is sustenance. We don't press on because praying or reading Scripture makes us right before God or removes our guilt. We press on because these practices are means of caring for ourselves spiritually, in the same way that eating food is a means of caring for ourselves physically.

We need Scripture in the same way we need regular meals. In times of physical sickness, it's especially important to eat nourishing food in easily digestible forms. Likewise, those times when we feel spiritually weak is often when we most need to be fed by "every word that comes from the mouth of the LORD."

This week you will brainstorm ways you can vary your approach to spiritual disciplines and focus on routines that are easy to carry. For example, you might switch to reading an easier version of the Bible, such as the Christian Standard Bible version or The Message, for a time. Consider listening to short podcasts to help you stay in the Word when reading feels too difficult. It might help to remember that the Spirit intercedes for you when you do not know how to pray. Try listening to praise and worship music or sermons on your commute. Or, the first time you reach for your phone each morning this week, play a Bible verse or passage on audio for five minutes.

Start with just one easily digestible means of practicing spiritual disciplines that might help you stay connected to God this week. Small moments with God often multiply over time into a renewed fervor to seek him.

GOSPEL SPOTLIGHT

If dry seasons have left you struggling with guilt and shame, remember that spiritual disciplines are not a means of righteousness. They are spiritual sources of nourishment that God has graciously given us. We are wise to eat our fill in the knowledge that our spiritual disciplines do not make us more righteous than we already are in Christ.

ACTION AND APPLICATION

Spiritual: Do spiritual disciplines feel easy or difficult in your current season of life? List any circumstances that have pulled you toward or away from Scripture and prayer in the past week.

Emotional: In what ways, if any, does your emotional state dictate whether or not you spend time with God? Which emotions, if any, pull you toward or away from Scripture and prayer?

Physical: Hunger pangs remind us of our need for physical nourishment. This week use hunger as a cue to remind you of your need for spiritual nourishment. Meditate on Deuteronomy 8:3 each time you eat a meal this week.

Relational: It's important to have people in our lives who can care for us when we feel spiritually weak. Who can pray for you, read Scripture with you, and encourage you when connecting with God feels difficult?

GUIDED JOURNALING

Brainstorm a list of easily digestible means of practicing spiritual disciplines that might help you stay connected to God during your current season of life.

WEEK 8
SILENCE IS COSTLY

> As long as you keep secrets and suppress information, you are
> fundamentally at war with yourself.
>
> *Bessel A. van der Kolk*

People say things in counseling that they don't say anywhere else.
I (Esther) consider it a privilege that people entrust me with
information they haven't openly talked about elsewhere. In fact,
I think it's accurate to say people sometimes come to counseling for this very purpose. Sometimes people confess secret sins.
Other times they share about suffering that feels shameful to
admit. Counseling provides a setting for people to pour out their
souls and share the most vulnerable parts of their lives.

As people open up about their pain, I sometimes notice a
visible shift in their countenance. A weight lifts from their soul.
How is this possible? It feels like I've done and said very little.
All I've done is listened, asked a few gentle questions, and honored their story. All this can create a safe place for secrets to be
brought into the light. Many times, people do not need answers
or advice to find emotional and spiritual healing. People often
experience newfound restoration and peace by simply breaking
their silence.

Rest is not just for our bodies. It's also for our hearts and our
minds. Our bodies could be lying on a resort beach, taking in
a beautiful view, sipping a cold beverage, and all the while our

minds and our souls are at war within us. We experience restlessness inside of ourselves when we wrestle through the weight of our sin and suffering on our own. We need a rest that goes beyond the physical. Scripture shows us that one way we experience this rest is through bringing our sins and sufferings into the light. **Scripture teaches us not to keep silent about our sin.** Covering up our sin is costly. Psalm 32 describes the impact of unspoken sin on King David's body and mind: "For when I kept silent, my bones wasted away through my groaning all day long. For day and night your hand was heavy upon me; my strength was dried up as by the heat of summer" (3–4). David made the choice to acknowledge his sin before God, and the Lord forgave the iniquity of his sin (3–5). The same is true for us. When we go to God and confess our sins, we experience rest within our souls.

Scripture encourages us not to keep silent about our suffering. In the midst of his suffering, as his friends admonish him to cease his complaints and to simply trust God, Job declares, "Therefore I will not keep silent; I will speak out in the anguish of my spirit, I will complain in the bitterness of my soul" (Job 7:11 NIV). Job gives free utterance to his complaints (Job 10:1), a practice also modeled in the Psalms. In his book *Dark Clouds, Deep Mercy*, Mark Vroegop describes how speaking the specifics of our suffering to God in this way protects us from bitterness, sharpens our prayers, and draws us closer to God.[2]

We all have parts of our lives that are hard to speak about. Many things we go through should not be broadcasted to the world, but most things we go through should be shared with at least one person. What are you keeping silent about? Are unspoken sins or sufferings leading to restlessness in your heart and mind?

GOSPEL SPOTLIGHT

No one is safer to go to with your sins and sufferings than Jesus. He can sympathize with your suffering (Hebrews 4:15). While you were still his enemy, he died for you (Romans 5:10). He deals gently with all who come to him (Hebrews 5:2).

ACTION AND APPLICATION

Spiritual: Silence has a costly effect on the state of our souls. What do you need to confess or share transparently with someone? Talking to a biblical counselor is a good option.

Emotional: Sharing about sin and suffering can lessen the emotional weight of your circumstances. Think back to a time when talking to someone about a struggle helped you feel better.

Physical: Psalm 32:3 says, "When I kept silent, my bones wasted away." Keeping our deepest sins and sufferings to ourselves can affect our physical bodies. Write down any ways you notice this happening to you.

Relational: Write down the name of a trustworthy friend. Take time this week to meet with this friend and share about a struggle you are carrying.

GUIDED JOURNALING

Journal through one area of suffering or sin you are keeping inside. Write about it in great detail. Share what you have written with God. Consider sharing what you have written with a friend or biblical counselor.

WEEK 9
STEWARD YOUR ATTENTION

Our thoughts are vanity, his thoughts are precious.

C. H. Spurgeon

Standing up in front of my computer screen, I (Eliza) let out an exhausted complaint to my husband. "We've seen a year's worth of bad news in just four months!" His response? "And we're not even halfway through this year!"

It's safe to say no matter what city, state, or country you are currently reading this from, you may have had a similar feeling about the year 2020. As if a global pandemic that made us all shelter in place was not enough, news highlighting the systemic issues of racial injustice led to mass protests and riots. Sprinkle in headlines of murder hornets, a contentious election, destructive fires, and a suffocating sandstorm, and it's hard to think of anything positive.

It's no exaggeration to say everyone carried around varying levels of anxiety that year. Our thoughts were bombarded with worst-case scenarios. The prevalence of bad news even began to invade our sleep, and the terms *corona-dreams* and *COVID-nightmares* were coined to describe an experience many shared in 2020.

You may not be having a repeat of 2020, but circumstances can easily become overwhelming, leaving you with a fragile mental bandwidth. Maybe someone said something to or about you and you can't shake the comment. Perhaps a misunderstanding at work has left you with lingering feelings of frustration. Maybe you are overwhelmed by financial stress and feel like looming bills are the only thing you think about. Possibly a strained relationship is leaving you feeling hopeless. What is the situation you find yourself rehearsing over and over in your thoughts?

Here's an important exercise you can use as a believer when circumstances seem to dominate your thinking. You can practice paying attention. Practice thinking. As we discussed in Week 4, where you focus your attention is key, and biblical meditation is one way to help you direct your thinking. Another practice is to make conscious decisions about your attention right in the midst of distressing moments. During moments of stress, resolve to pay attention to truth. Recall God's relevant promises for your present circumstances.

In counseling terms, this is called mindfulness. In biblical terms it is to "take every thought captive" (2 Corinthians 10:5). A phrase a colleague shared with me described it as "stewarding your attention." In simple terms it's noticing what you are thinking about and deciding if that's what should captivate your mind. It's an in-the-moment reorientation of your thinking.

When you steward your attention, you decide what you will focus on. You can choose to linger on the trouble and distress or fix your mind on the promises and hope you have from God. Scripture gives instruction on what we need to think about and how important our thoughts are (see Psalm 1:2; 19:14; Proverbs 23:7; Isaiah 26:3; Romans 12:2; Philippians 4:8).

Taking care of yourself starts in the privacy of your mind. This week make it a priority to pay attention to what you are giving your attention to.

GOSPEL SPOTLIGHT

As a believer you have been given the mind of Christ. He has secured abundant blessings for you that are unchangeable no matter the circumstances you face (1 Corinthians 2:9–16). Let this truth fill your mind this week.

ACTION AND APPLICATION

Spiritual: Read through the Scriptures listed above. Choose one to meditate on more intentionally. Refer back to Week 4 for help with meditation.

Emotional: How are your thoughts impacting your emotions? The next time you have a thought that seems significant, take note of how it makes you feel.

Physical: Consider placing physical reminders of God's promises in places where you can see them as you go about your day. Start with the verses above. Write them out on cards or sticky notes and put them in places that will catch your attention.

Relational: How you think about someone flavors how you feel about them. This week seek to be more thankful about the relationships in your life. Take some time to share thoughts of gratitude with one or two people for whom you are thankful for the relationship you share.

GUIDED JOURNALING

Changing your thoughts can be difficult, but God does not leave you alone in this. He is able and ready to help you steward your attention in ways that reflect a mind that is set on him. In your journal, finish this sentence as a first step in seeking God regarding your attention:

God, I need help changing these thoughts . . .

SECTION 2
PHYSICAL LIFE

WEEK 10
BEYOND SOUL NOURISHING

> God does not bypass the body in the sanctification process.
>
> *Michael R. Emlet*

When we began to brainstorm the idea of this book, the topic of self-care was gaining significant momentum. It was not just the healthcare industry promoting the importance of caring for oneself. Businesses began to see the value of helping employees avoid burnout by prioritizing self-care.

Practices such as requiring employees to use personal time off (PTO) or rewarding employees who participate in physical exercise have become part of many companies' policies. Clif Bar & Company gives their employees thirty minutes of paid personal time every day to stretch, take a walk, or run.[3] Other companies offer mental health days for workers to do whatever is needed to attend to their total well-being.[4] These initiatives are becoming more commonplace.

Self-care has also gone digital. It's not hard to find websites and apps focused on self-care. Some apps give reminders to drink water, take deep breaths, or simply stand up and stretch. You can find endless articles and blogs addressing more holistic personal care that engages physical, mental, and emotional health.

For Christians, when it comes to addressing personal care, the emphasis is mainly on spiritual well-being. We focus on how we are doing in the sanctification process and what we must do to better nurture our eternal souls. However, in an effort to focus on being spiritually nourished, care for the whole person can be inadvertently sidelined. We don't see skipping meals, avoiding exercise, or neglecting healthy amounts of sleep as a problem. This sends a message that the only thing that matters is our spiritual health. But Jesus doesn't ignore the needs of the body.

In Matthew 15:32, Jesus goes beyond caring for people's spiritual needs. The crowds were with him all day hearing his teaching. What else could they need in life than to sit and learn from the Son of God? We could think that this would be enough for anyone. But take note of what Jesus does: "[He] called his disciples to him and said, 'I have compassion on the crowd because they have been with me now three days and have nothing to eat. And I am unwilling to send them away hungry, lest they faint on the way.'"

Jesus went beyond nourishing their souls. He had compassion on the crowd regarding their physical needs. He did not want them to go away hungry or potentially fainting on their way home. Jesus showed us that our bodily needs matter. In fact, neglecting our physical needs can actually make it more difficult to respond to and embrace spiritual teaching.

GOSPEL SPOTLIGHT

Following Jesus does not mean you need to choose between caring for your soul or caring for your body. Rest in the knowledge that taking care of your body matters to Jesus. He loves and cares for all of you and gave his life to bring redemption to every part of you.

ACTION AND APPLICATION

Spiritual: Take time to pray about how you care for yourself in all areas. Ask God to help you view your bodily needs in the same way he does. Confess to him any wrong views of caring for yourself.

Emotional: Consider how your physical health is connected to your emotional health. Write down one change you feel you need to make to your physical health habits to improve your emotional health.

Physical: Commit to focusing on your physical needs this week. Consider taking a walk daily, doing some morning stretches, getting more sleep, cutting out unhealthy eating, or making any needed medical appointments.

Relational: Bring a friend into your commitment to focusing on your physical needs this week. Share with them the changes you are implementing and ask them to join you.

GUIDED JOURNALING

Read about bullet journaling in the appendix. This quick method of journaling is a helpful way to organize your thoughts. Bullet journal the areas of physical health that you need to focus on this week. Revisit this journal entry every day this week. Add to it as needed.

WEEK 11
STOP PUSHING THROUGH

How differently does the Holy Spirit work from the devil. While Satan accuses only to bring despair, bondage, and striving, the Holy Spirit convicts only to bring comfort, freedom, and rest.

Roy and Revel Hession

Grab a pencil and take a short quiz:

I feel exhausted or drained more often than not. Y N

It's hard to believe that my work is meaningful or making a difference. Y N

I tend to complain about work and often have a negative attitude. Y N

I've noticed an increase in unexplained physical symptoms. Y N

I feel I am achieving less than I should. Y N

I'm unable to rest, relax, or calm down when not working. Y N

I'm not performing at work as well as I did in the past. Y N

I've noticed an increase in arguments at work or at
home. Y N

I feel detached from God or unable to pray. Y N

I feel like nobody understands what I'm going
through. Y N

I struggle to concentrate or solve problems. Y N

I'm often angry or irritable. Y N

I grow more apathetic about work, faith, or family as
time goes on. Y N

While this quiz is not an official diagnostic tool, each statement
represents a common sign of burnout. The more times you answered yes, the more likely you are starting to burn out. Burnout
happens when you push through high levels of stress for long
periods of time without a break. It's associated with serious physical, emotional, and spiritual problems such as those mentioned
in the quiz.

Pushing through stress and the first signs of burnout can seem
like a more spiritual choice than pausing to rest. It's easy to ignore
the exhaustion and physical symptoms. The negativity, detach-
ment, and cynicism may go unnoticed. We keep going even when
these symptoms arise because we take seriously the call of "always
abounding in the work of the Lord" (1 Corinthians 15:58) and to
devote ourselves to good works (Titus 3:14). Verses like these seem
to imply a ceaseless drive toward caring for others. What we fail
to account for is the fact that burnout has the potential to stop us
in our tracks. It can temporarily, and in severe cases permanently,
derail our ability to do good works at all.

Galatians 6:9 encourages us to work in such a way that we
do "not grow weary of doing good." At first glance, this verse
seems to encourage an attitude of pushing through, but take a

closer look. Notice that the concept of "weariness in doing good" is very similar to the experience of burnout, which is defined as a state of "exhaustion, negativity, and reduced effectiveness at work." Instead of automatically compelling us to work harder, this verse should lead us to consider an important question: What *level* of good works can we devote ourselves to over the course of a lifetime that will not yield weariness in doing good?

If we want to serve well throughout our lives, we will have to pace ourselves. We each need to assess an appropriate pace for ourselves, because we all have different capacities. Some of us can do more than others. A good question to start with might be, "Is my current pace sustainable?" Can you keep doing as much as you are doing over the next month? The next year? The next ten years? If the thought of sustaining your current pace for that long makes you feel a sense of dread or uneasiness, that is probably a sign you should slow down. It's a sign you may need to cut down on how much you are doing, a process we will discuss more in Week 22.

If we want to protect our bodies from serious harm that will impair our functioning, we will have to stop ignoring signs of burnout. The goal is not to avoid all stress. Mild to moderate levels of stress help us perform our jobs and life responsibilities at a higher level. The goal is to prevent stress from accumulating into a medical syndrome that has the potential to damage our bodies and erode our working capacity.

Are you exhausted? Increasingly negative and cynical? Struggling to perform well at work? You would be wise to listen to these important warning signs. Danger may lie ahead.

GOSPEL SPOTLIGHT

We sometimes push to the point of burnout because we believe God will be more pleased with us if we do more for him. Remind yourself that because of Christ's work on your behalf, there is no amount of work you can do that will make God more pleased with you than he already is.

ACTION AND APPLICATION

Spiritual: It's easy to come up with spiritual excuses for overworking to the point of burnout. Do you ever find yourself justifying dangerous levels of overwork with Scripture passages? If so, which ones?

Emotional: One reason burnout goes undetected is because it leaves people too emotionally depleted to assess their current state. Consider if this might be the case for you.

Physical: Make a list of any physical symptoms you have experienced over the last month. For each symptom, ask yourself, "What is this symptom telling me? What might this symptom be warning me about?"

Relational: Review the results of your quiz with someone you trust. Ask them to go over your answers and give you honest feedback on whether or not they think you answered accurately. Have an honest discussion with them of what may need to change in your life to prevent burnout.

GUIDED JOURNALING

The sooner you take steps to manage burnout, the more effectively and quickly your body, mind, and soul will revert back to a healthy state. Prevention is always more effective than treating burnout that's already out of control. What symptoms of burnout are you currently experiencing? What steps could you take to prevent these symptoms from progressing?

WEEK 12
BECOME LIKE A CHILD

Play is really the work of childhood.

Fred Rogers

In Matthew 18, we read a story about Jesus, his disciples, and a little child. The disciples come to Jesus and ask, "Who is the greatest in the kingdom of heaven?" (Matthew 18:1). We can imagine they hoped he would name one of them. As those closest to Jesus, the disciples were doing important work. Surely, he would choose them to hold places of highest honor (see Matthew 20:21). In answer to their question, Jesus calls over a small, seemingly insignificant child and says, "Whoever humbles himself like this child is the greatest in the kingdom of heaven" (Matthew 18:4).

The humility Jesus mentions in this verse has much to do with social status. Children have little standing in society. While adults often concern themselves with accomplishments, productivity, and being great in the kingdom of God, children are most concerned about the work of playing and imagining. Children don't seek important positions; instead, they approach the world with a sense of wonder. Children draw outside the lines, make massive messes in the kitchen, and spend hours living in make-believe worlds. They sing songs, dance, tell terrible jokes, and try new and silly things.

When I (Esther) was a child, I liked to climb trees, walk in creeks, ride my bike, and catch fireflies. I spent hours reading fiction and playing in the pool with my friends. It never crossed my mind to feel guilty about spending my time in these ways, because life was more about being than accomplishing. As a child, life was more focused on relationships than work, more grounded in enjoying God's world than trying to become the greatest. I like to believe that when Jesus calls us to become like a child, he is pulling us away from our need to prove ourselves toward a simpler way of life.

As adults, we tend to take ourselves too seriously. There's important work to be done, and we don't have time to bother with silly games. We are too busy working toward our next goal, contributing to the latest trending cause, and building up our résumés. Like the disciples, we approach Jesus and say, "Look, Jesus, do you see how great I am?" In response, Jesus gently pulls us away from our scrambling and says, "Humble yourself like a child."

One way to become like a child is to reintroduce play into your life if this has been an area of neglect. Think about the last time you did something for the pure enjoyment of it. When was the last time you indulged in a hobby? Do you ever take time to laugh, recreate, or enjoy activities that don't feel productive? The world tells us that hard work, advancement, and public praise will prove our greatness. Jesus says that greatness comes not through important positions or achievements, but through modeling the simple humility of a child who wants nothing more than to play the morning away.

Become like a child and regain your sense of wonder. If you aren't sure where to start, remember some of the activities you used to enjoy when you were growing up. It can also help to think about hobbies and interests you have in the back of your mind that you won't let yourself try. Many of us are very out of practice when it comes to playing and imagining, but it's never too late to relearn how to savor life again.

GOSPEL SPOTLIGHT

The urge to prove ourselves can also surface as we consider our salvation. We want to work toward right standing with Christ instead of receiving it as a free gift of grace. If you struggle in this area, close your eyes and imagine receiving God's righteousness with the unabashed joy of a child opening a longed-for gift at Christmas.

ACTION AND APPLICATION

Spiritual: It's easy to spend our days scrambling to become the greatest, just like the disciples. Read Matthew 18 and prayerfully ask the Lord to show you how you have embraced the mindset of the disciples in wanting to become great.

Emotional: One of the primary emotions that holds us back from engaging in hobbies and play is guilt. If this is the case for you, how might Jesus's invitation to become like a child change your perspective?

Physical: Activities that encourage physical fitness can be a great way to start playing again. What is one activity you would like to try that is both enjoyable and good for your body?

Relational: If you have children or work with children, take some time to observe them playing. Journal about what you learn.

GUIDED JOURNALING

Do you have any hobbies or playful interests? Brainstorm a list of fifteen to thirty ideas. Write them out as fast as you can, and don't censor yourself. Pick just one of them to try this week.

WEEK 13
ATTEND TO YOUR BODY

I am not the owner of my body, but I am the caretaker, or
manager, of it. The word for manager in the Bible is steward.
Taking care of my body is an issue of spiritual stewardship.

Rick Warren

For the third week in a row I (Eliza) had a stabbing pain in my
neck whenever I turned my head to the right. Since most of the
work I do has me looking straight in front of me at a person or
a computer, I managed the pain by simply avoiding turning my
head. Then one day my face started to go numb on one side.
This concerned me enough to finally go to the doctor. It would
take the fear of losing feeling in my face to get me to pay attention to the symptoms that had previously nudged me day by day.

I'm ashamed to say I have actually cared for my vehicles better than my body. If I hear a concerning noise or notice a change
in performance, I take my car to the mechanic. The thought of
being stranded on a DC highway definitely fuels my attentive
response. I also just know that if I take good care of my car, I
reap the benefits of dependability.

Our bodies are the unique vehicles that transport us through
life. There may be times we wouldn't mind a trade-in, but the
fact is, our bodies will be with us for the rest of our lives here on
earth. Since that's true, it's important to attend to our bodies.

We are embodied souls. We love God and love our neighbor with our bodies. We worship with our bodies. Our bodies are temples of the Holy Spirit and are a means to glorify God (1 Corinthians 6:19–20). As we face suffering, the life of Jesus is revealed in our bodies (2 Corinthians 4:10). The body has an important part to play in the believer's life.

When your body communicates to you through symptoms, listen to it. Staying present with your body requires you to notice it. Take a moment right now and notice what you feel in your body. How is your posture? Are you hungry? Thirsty? Is there stress or tension anywhere in your body? Scan your body and notice what it is telling you. Stop reading now and give yourself a minute to pay attention to your body.

Are you mentally exhausted? Do your thoughts seem scattered or troublesome? Are you discouraged or weary in your spirit? Do you feel spiritually dry? Consider how the care or lack of care for your body may be contributing to these things. What choices do you make daily that reflect care or neglect of your body?

Our physical health impacts our spiritual, mental, and relational health. We cannot separate our bodies from the rest of our lives. Ignoring the nurturing of our bodies will negatively impact every part of life. Every day we make decisions that determine what kind of care we will give to our bodies. Will we attend to our bodies through adequate sleep, good nutrition, or regular exercise? Or will we neglect the routine maintenance that keeps our bodies running well?

GOSPEL SPOTLIGHT

The ability to love God with our heart, soul, mind, and strength flows out of a life surrendered to God. As Christians, we have a God who knows our frame and all of its frailty and reminds us that he is the source of grace and strength (2 Corinthians 12:9).

ACTION AND APPLICATION

Spiritual: Read 1 Corinthians 6:19–20. How do these verses encourage you in prioritizing the care and attention of your body?

Emotional: What emotional struggles are you facing that might be linked to the way you have treated your body?

Physical: Do the Body Scan Activity found in the appendix. What do you notice? Consider what sort of care your body needs.

Relational: How does the way you treat your body impact your relationships? If you are unsure, consider asking those closest to you for input.

GUIDED JOURNALING

This week choose how you will attend to your body. Write down ways you can begin caring for your body better. Consider what habits need to be removed or what new habits you need to begin.

WEEK 14
PRIORITIZING MEDICAL CARE

> Action expresses priorities.
>
> *Mahatma Gandhi*

According to a journal article titled "Why Do People Avoid Medical Care," 30 percent of people "avoid visiting their doctor when they suspect they should."[5] In other words, three out of ten people reading this book are ignoring a nagging feeling that they should seek medical care. Raise your hand if you are one of them. Unfortunately, the other 70 percent of you don't get a free pass. Raise your hand if it's been one or more years since you saw your doctor for a checkup. Three years? Five years? Ten years? I'll stop there.

My goal this week is to convince you of the importance of regular medical care. True, this isn't the most exciting topic. This might even be a touchy subject for some. Perhaps someone has encouraged or nagged you to go to the doctor for ages and you just don't want to. So far, your stubbornness has prevailed.

There are so many reasons *not* to go to the doctor. You might assume that symptoms will go away on their own. Or perhaps you have had a bad experience with doctors in the past. Many people face barriers related to insurance, finances, transportation, schedules, and childcare that make regular medical care difficult. Other times, it's hard to believe going to the doctor will make a difference. You've been dealing with your issue for so long, it seems pointless to keep trying to fix it. Maybe you are scared a doctor's appointment will reveal something serious. It's easier to not know.

Caring for our bodies often isn't pleasant. It requires time, energy, money, and going to uncomfortable offices. Due to my chronic illness, I (Esther) am intimately acquainted with how inconvenient it can be to maintain regular medical care. Most weeks, I attend at least one medical appointment, whether it's physical therapy, acupuncture, a primary care check-in, or a specialist appointment. These appointments are time consuming, and I would rather be doing something else. So, why do I go? I make the effort because I believe it is my responsibility to care for the body that God has given me.

My body is not my own (1 Corinthians 6:19–20). It does not belong to me. I believe God created my individual body to fulfill a specific role within the church body (Romans 12:4), and I am best equipped to fulfill that role when my body is functioning at its best. It's not that I don't have anything to offer when I am physically weak. Our weaknesses are part of what God uses for his glory (2 Corinthians 12:10). Even so, I have found that taking steps to address physical limitations equips me to serve in ways that would otherwise be impossible.

Step out of your comfort zone this week. Take care of that ongoing issue. Seek out preventative care. Your body is on loan from God. Are you treating it with the care it deserves?

GOSPEL SPOTLIGHT

Jesus died for our souls and our bodies. His sacrifice ensures that our bodies will one day be raised up, free from sickness and pain. Caring for the health of our bodies in the present points toward the full redemption and glorification we will one day experience.

ACTION AND APPLICATION

Spiritual: Does the way you seek medical care reflect the fact that your body does not belong to you? If not, what needs to change?

Emotional: Journal through any fears or concerns you have about going to the doctor. Do any of your fears surprise you or stand out to you?

Physical: What physical health issues, if any, have you been ignoring or just hoping will go away? Schedule a doctor's appointment this week for any physical issues you find. If you feel healthy, but haven't seen a doctor for over two years, schedule a checkup.

Relational: Avoiding the doctor can lead to relational conflict, especially within marriages. If you have been ignoring someone's encouragement to visit the doctor, ask this person to explain any reasons for concern. Listen without interrupting, and try to see things from an outside perspective.

GUIDED JOURNALING

Finish this thought: I will follow through on the appointment I scheduled because . . .

WEEK 15
HABITS OF EATING AND DRINKING

What if exercise and discipline in eating isn't as much about
physical health as about honoring the God who made us?

Gary L. Thomas

My favorite bad habit when I (Esther) am stressed is to drink
way too much coffee. For me, coffee is liquid comfort. I sit at my
computer typing and drink cup after cup after cup. At the same
time, stress and overwork lead me to forget to eat and drink
water. I'm well aware this combination of habits is a recipe for
disaster, but awareness doesn't always stop me from repeating
this pattern.

Drinking too much coffee may seem like an innocuous
habit, but small choices add up. Too much coffee can make me
anxious and jittery. Coffee fuels me into overwork for a time and
then leads me to crash later. It's not uncommon for me to make
it halfway through the day without drinking any water and sud-
denly realize I am dehydrated. When my body is unhappy, I start
to feel irritable, which can lead me to lash out at people. My
emotional state, physical health, work habits, and relationships
are all impacted when I am not mindful of what I choose to put
into my body.

I'm not alone in using harmful eating and drinking habits
to cope when life is busy or stressful. Consider your own life for
a moment. What sort of relationship do you have with food? It's

easy to misuse food to self-medicate emotional pain or drive us into overwork. For some, overindulging in sweets can be used to numb feelings of depression. Undereating and restricting calories help others regain a sense of control. Binge drinking is a common coping strategy for forgetting problems, if only for a night. Other people find themselves idolizing clean diets or consuming all the wrong things at all the wrong times.

It's easy to avoid dealing with these bad habits and ignore the fact that even mundane choices such as the food we eat and the beverages we drink can impact not only our own health but also our ability to serve others. In 1 Corinthians 10, Paul addresses the issue of whether believers should eat food that has been sacrificed to idols. In making this decision, believers are instructed to keep God's glory and the good of others in mind. Whether they eat or drink, or whatever they do, God's glory is the highest goal (1 Corinthians 10:31). Their decisions about what they eat should be based not on seeking their own good, "but the good of many, so that they may be saved" (1 Corinthians 10:33 NIV).

As believers, our bodies belong to Jesus. We honor God through our eating and drinking when we remember that what we put into our bodies is not just about us. The way we eat should seek not just our own good, but the good of those around us. Binge drinking, idolizing food, and eating in other sinful ways can harm our bodies, impair our ability to serve, and hinder our relationship with God. Caring for our bodies through healthy eating can improve our health and increase our ability to do kingdom work. While drinking one more cup of coffee may serve my desire for comfort, stopping my work to drink water is one small choice toward fueling my body for the good of others.

GOSPEL SPOTLIGHT

This week allow your physical need for food and water to remind you of your spiritual need for Christ. Jesus says, "I am the bread of life; whoever comes to me shall not hunger, and whoever believes in me shall never thirst" (John 6:35).

ACTION AND APPLICATION

Spiritual: Identify one specific way you can bring God glory and seek other people's good through your eating and drinking choices.

Emotional: The next time you use binge-eating, restricting food, consuming alcohol, or other similar habits to cope with difficult emotions, take a moment to notice your feelings. Say out loud, "I'm feeling _____." Then, instead of using food to cope, seek out God to meet your emotional needs.

Physical: List one food or drink you consume in unhealthy or unhelpful ways and how it negatively impacts your body.

Relational: Do you ever become irritable or easily annoyed when you indulge in bad eating or drinking habits? How does this impact the people around you?

GUIDED JOURNALING

Write out an action plan for how you will implement healthier eating and drinking habits this year. Identify one bad habit you want to break. What steps will you take to break this habit? Identify one good habit you want to develop. What steps will you take to put this habit into action?

WEEK 16
THE ROLE OF MEDICATION

> Christian liberty must be taught and believed if men are to . . .
> enjoy peace of mind.
>
> *John Calvin*

When physical or mental health struggles impact our functioning, it can be difficult to know what to do. The easiest course of action is to hope these problems will go away on their own. For many of us, going to the doctor, seeking out a counselor, or considering medication are seen as a last resort. The prospect of taking medication tends to be especially terrifying to people. When I counsel people through this decision, I often hear concerns such as these:

> "Taking medication would mean admitting that I actually do have depression, and that terrifies me."

> "I shouldn't need help from a pill just to make it through the day without falling apart."

> "I talked to my pastor, and he is very cautious about medication. He wants me to pursue biblically focused care."

> "I'm scared. Scared of side effects. Scared that it won't work. Scared I will be on it for the rest of my life."

How about you? Has the possibility of needing to take medication been presented to you? Are you struggling with what to do? Are you tempted to immediately take this option off the table? It's common to avoid medication for a variety of reasons. In the case of mental health struggles, well-meaning people in our lives might be unsure if medication is a biblical option. Medication for certain physical struggles can also be avoided at times out of shame or associated stigma.

Charles Hodges presents the following framework for understanding medication: "Taking medication for depression and any other cause is a Romans 14 issue of Christian liberty . . . since the Bible says nothing about any particular drug or medication, it is the privilege of every believer to make their own mind up about it."[6] Medication for both physical and mental struggles is an issue requiring wisdom and discernment, and Christians are free to make different choices.

In making decisions about Christian liberties, Scripture instructs us to take other people into account (Romans 15:1–2). Depending on the situation, exercising your liberty to take medication could either positively or negatively impact your family, friends, coworkers, or employees. At times, taking medication can be a way to steward both your body and the medical resources God has provided. Other times, it can have unhelpful side effects or help you to avoid dealing with the root of your problems. In these cases, medication may not be the best option.

In the context of self-care, medication can be a gift from God that allows us to live at higher levels of functioning. Many people experience relief from their symptoms when they take medication for both physical and emotional struggles. This allows them to more adequately fulfill important roles and responsibilities in life. In some cases, medication can improve people's ability to pray, read Scripture, and connect with God by providing much-needed physical relief or mental clarity. As you consider if medication might play a role in your personal self-care, consider how these potential benefits may help both you and those you serve.

GOSPEL SPOTLIGHT

Christian liberties flow out of the freedom we have in Christ. Christ has freed us for the purpose of serving one another in love (Galatians 5:13).

ACTION AND APPLICATION

Spiritual: Read Romans 14, which describes how to approach Christian liberties. Ask God to reveal whether medication would be a good option for you and your current situation.

Emotional: The decision to take medication can bring many fears to the surface. Fears about side effects. Fears that you might be crazy. If you are considering medication, talk to someone about your concerns.

Physical: Even medication for physical ailments can be stigmatized or avoided for various reasons. Do you have any physical symptoms that are impairing your functioning? Write down one physical symptom you might consider taking medication for.

Relational: Are you experiencing any symptoms that make it difficult for you to fulfill roles or responsibilities in your life? Are mental or medical symptoms negatively impacting your relationships? Medication could be a way to love people in your life by helping you become more physically and emotionally available.

GUIDED JOURNALING

Many people face the decision of whether or not they should take medication at least once in their lifetime. If you are facing this decision right now, journal through some of your motivations. Are you being motivated by anxiety, pride, or fear of man? Or are you being motivated by love for others and a desire to please God in your decision?

WEEK 17
A BODY OF EMOTIONS

Your body is the vehicle through which the passion of your
soul flows.

Alasdair Groves and Winston T. Smith

We first learn about emotions from our families. For most of us,
our parents didn't sit us down and teach us all there is to know
about our feelings. Instead, as children we implicitly learned
about emotions as we observed the ways our parents displayed
emotions and responded to our emotions.

Take Jean for example. At the age of ten, Jean's dad was diagnosed with Lou Gehrig's disease, and for years the family didn't
tell a single person. Her father hid his symptoms for as long
as possible and continued on with life as though nothing had
changed. Jean never once saw her father become upset. He never
displayed sadness, fear, or any other emotions about his diagno-
sis. Jean learned to bury her emotions at all costs. To this day, she
never shares her feelings with anyone.

Brian, on the other hand, grew up in an overly emotional
environment. Both of his parents expressed their emotions in
ways that negatively impacted the family. His mother struggled
with depression and would spend hours crying in the kitchen
every day. His father had an anger problem. When something
went wrong at work, he would come home agitated and yell
the moment something annoyed him. Brian learned to spew his
emotions without thought, a practice he continues as an adult.

When we fail to steward our emotions well, our relationships suffer. Suppressing or avoiding our emotions hinders our ability to be close to people. When we emote without thought of how our choices impact others, we damage relational bonds. Only when we learn to identify, engage, and respond to our emotions in healthy ways can they help us form connections with others.[7] Give this a try right now. What emotion are you feeling right now? If you can't identify something specific in this moment, think of an emotion you felt at some point in the last day. Take a close look at this emotion. What situation or other trigger contributed to this feeling? Did you suppress or over emote this feeling? Or, did you share it with someone in a way that helped you connect with that person?

Scripture instructs us to weep with those who weep and laugh with those who laugh (Romans 12:15). This exchange of emotions leads to closeness and community. When you share your feelings with someone else, your bond with that person grows. Emotions can also draw us toward God. Distress, hurt, and mistreatment lead us to prayerful cries for help to a God who hears (Exodus 22:23; Psalm 18:6; 34:18). Joy, gratitude, and wonder compel us to praise (Psalm 8:3; 47:1; 118:1). When we steward our emotions well, they become a catalyst for connection.

What does all this have to do with our bodies? To share what you feel requires the ability to identify your emotions. Many times, our bodies give us the first hint that certain emotions are rising to the surface before our feelings hit our conscious awareness. Fear tightens our chest. Joy brightens our eyes. Our faces grow hot with anger. Sadness is felt as an indescribable pit deep in our stomachs. Pause from this reading right now. Draw your attention to your body. What physical sensations do you feel? Are they alerting you to any emotions?

Emotional health is too often neglected in the Christian life. Focusing on this area can help us grow in personal sanctification and in our relationships. As you identify what you are feeling, you can share your heart with those around you. As you grow more aware of how your feelings are connected to your circumstances, you are better able to respond in God-honoring ways. One practical way to grow in emotional awareness is to pay more attention to how emotions reside in your body.

GOSPEL SPOTLIGHT

One day we will experience the wonder of emotions untainted by suffering or sin. God will wipe every tear from our eyes and we will be free from all mourning, sadness, and pain. We can rejoice and be glad even now as we anticipate the eternity with God that Christ has bought for us.

ACTION AND APPLICATION

Spiritual: Reflect on what you learned growing up about emotions. What experiences led to these beliefs?

Emotional: To help you grow in your ability to identify what you are feeling, journal through a day in your life with a specific focus on your emotions. Explain what happened. What did you feel in response to what happened? How did you express or act on your emotions?

Physical: The next time you experience a strong emotion, pay close attention to your body. What clues does your body give you about what you are feeling?

Relationships: Think of an important relationship in your life that feels distant. Make a conscious effort this week to humbly and graciously share what you are feeling with this person.

GUIDED JOURNALING

Journal your thoughts on this statement: Christians should make an effort to become emotionally healthy, which includes being more aware of their emotions as they experience them.

WEEK 18
LOVING OTHERS WITH YOUR HEALTH

Pay mind to your own life, your own health, and wholeness. A
bleeding heart is of no help to anyone if it bleeds to death.

Frederick Buechner

A microscopic invisible enemy was terrorizing countries across
the world. The year was 2020, and COVID-19, also known
to the world as the novel coronavirus, was on a rampage. As it
spread across the globe, the aggressively contagious disease was
the topic of everyone's conversation. Everyone was impacted.

The most dangerous thing about the virus was not how sick
people became. In fact, most people did not get that sick at all.
The World Health Organization (WHO) stated that 80 percent
of all cases were mild.[8] Not moderate, not severe, not lethal, but
mild. The most dangerous aspect of the virus was how rapidly
it spread, making it challenging to contain once an outbreak
happened. While most people would recover, the risk was in the
susceptibility of everyone. People who didn't know they were
sick could carry the virus to those at greater risk. People with
preexisting health issues or weakened immune systems were
deeply impacted by choices of the healthier population.

What does the coronavirus pandemic have to do with self-
care? Self-care is not just about you. This really is not a new concept. When reading about self-care you often hear the metaphor
of the oxygen masks in an airplane. Put your mask on first. You

can't care for another person if you have not first taken care of yourself. The COVID-19 outbreak shed new light on that reality.

Caring for yourself can be a way to care for others. If you avoid dealing with emotional struggles, it could impact those who count on your emotional stability. If you ignore your need for health care, those who depend on you could end up suffering as you juggle life with poor health. If you neglect your spiritual health, there is a potential risk to those who look to you for godly direction and leadership. You may not find yourself in the midst of a pandemic, but there may be ways your lack of attention to your needs is putting others at greater risk.

Romans 15 can help us think about this. "Now we who are strong have an obligation to bear the weaknesses of those without strength, and not to please ourselves. Each one of us is to please his neighbor for his good, to build him up. For even Christ did not please himself" (Romans 15:1–3 CSB). The context of this passage is regarding the conscience of a person as it relates to meat sacrificed to idols. But the principle here is that Christians are called to consider others in the actions and choices they make. Sometimes the decision to please and do good to your neighbor will mean being a good steward of your own health.

Though I (Eliza) stayed well during those first scary months of the pandemic, I took precautions as if I could be sick. I got extra sleep, washed my hands more attentively, wore a face mask, and stayed at home. Sure, I was caring for myself, but as I took care of myself, the health of others was always in view. What a global health crisis taught me is just how much attention and care toward myself can truly be a means of loving others.

GOSPEL SPOTLIGHT

If this week's entry convicted you about how your lack of care for yourself may be impacting others, you are not alone. It is incredibly easy to put off self-care. Take a moment and be honest before the Lord about where repentance or change is needed. Rest in the reality of the abundant forgiveness and grace available to you in Jesus.

ACTION AND APPLICATION

Spiritual: List two or three people close to you who are impacted by your spiritual health. With these people in mind, make efforts this week to adjust your schedule or routine to protect your personal time with the Lord.

Emotional: How is your emotional health impacting others around you? Have you considered seeing a counselor to help you attend to your emotional needs? Revisit Week 6 if you have any hesitations on this.

Physical: Are you neglecting physical needs in your own life that could impact the well-being of others? Embrace the concept that caring for yourself is caring for others, and attend to those needs this week.

Relational: Think of the relationships in your life that would benefit from you taking better care of yourself. Let the importance of these relationships motivate you to take better care of your own health.

GUIDED JOURNALING

Consider someone whose emotional, physical, or spiritual health is dependent on or influenced by you. How does your neglect of self-care impact this person?

SECTION 3
A PURPOSEFUL LIFE

WEEK 19

TWO TRUTHS TO START EACH DAY

In the morning when I rise, give me Jesus.

African-American hymn

Everyone has an approach to starting the day. For some it may include some form of regular exercise, time with the Lord, or calendar assessment. For others it might be the simple "nothing-before-coffee" routine. In this section of the book as we focus on the importance of living a purposeful life, there are two unchangeable truths to keep in mind: (1) We need help, and (2) Jesus is available to help us. These two truths are helpful in how you purposefully plan your life but are also beneficial in giving you a singular focus as you start each day. The singular focus is Jesus. Every day, every morning, we need Jesus.

Before you get too worried, I am not going to urge you to set a wake-up time, establish an eating or exercising regimen, or create a personal checklist of morning activities, though none of those are bad ideas. Instead, I want to help you see the value of recognizing your need to orient your heart to Jesus from the very moment you open your eyes.

There is abundant evidence proving that how we start our day impacts the remainder of the day. But you don't need the research to tell you that. You've probably had days when the alarm failed on the morning of a very important meeting or event and you rushed into the day in a panic. Or maybe you are a parent who was up all night with a newborn just to be jolted from sleep once again at the break of dawn. You drag yourself out of bed despite how ill-prepared you feel to face the day.

We all have days that start out rough, and we carry the impact into the rest of the morning or maybe the entire day. How we start our day affects the rest of our day, but what if we start our day with truth that can impact the rest of our lives?

The first truth is that we need help. There isn't a moment when help is not necessary in our lives. If we go back as far as Adam and Eve, we see we were created to be dependent. Since the garden we continue to need help, and God is the source of that help. In John 15:5, Jesus minces no words when he says, "Apart from me you can do nothing."

Have you ever wondered why our first parents doubted an all-providing God? Do you shake your head at the foolishness of their independent thinking? Before we self-righteously question them, we need to see how we do the same thing every day. We think we have what it takes to manage things. We may not say that outright, but we show it by our lack of dependence. The moment our eyelids open, we ought to acknowledge our need. By doing so, we position ourselves for the next important truth.

The second truth is that Jesus is available to help us. At the first inhale that we take from unconscious sleep to the reality of being awake, the Lord is there (Psalm 145:18). Before our feet move from our beds to touch the floor, he is our helper (Psalm 54:4). He watched us as we slept, and he will carry us into our day (Psalm 42:8). He is our provider, helper, and sustainer (Psalm 55:22). He has what we need for the day ahead (Philippians 4:19).

How you start your day orients your heart. If you can take hold of these truths at the start of your day, they in turn will direct your entire life. Begin this week with these two truths and allow them to guide you as you go about all you have to do.

GOSPEL SPOTLIGHT

What a beautiful picture these two truths give us. They are unchangeable and eternal. The reality that we need help is set in the context that we have a Savior that promises to always be with us (Hebrews 13:5).

ACTION AND APPLICATION

Spiritual: Read Psalm 5:1–3 and Psalm 63:1–5. Write down how these verses encourage you to focus your first thoughts of the day on the Lord.

Emotional: Your feelings need instruction. If you start your day emotionally drained or down, instruct yourself with the truth of God's provision and care for you. How can these two truths change the way you feel about the day in front of you?

Physical: Notice how you physically feel in the morning. Are you carrying tension in your body before your day even starts? If so, spend a couple minutes each morning doing the breathing exercise (see appendix) while listening to Scripture. Consider using the same Scripture listed above.

Relational: The two truths shared this week are about more than self-care. They point to our primary need for a right relationship with God. If you are not living a life of total dependence on Jesus, take time now to confess your self-sufficiency. A right relationship with God is freely offered in Jesus. If you are unsure of your relationship with God talk to a trusted friend or pastor this week about it.

GUIDED JOURNALING

Start a bullet journal of ways you see the Lord's help every day. Review this list from time to time and add to it.

WEEK 20
LIVE WITH PURPOSE

It is wonderful what great strides can be made when there is a
resolute purpose behind them.

Winston Churchill

Sarah is a single woman and a seminary student paying her way
through school as she works part time as an intern at her church.
She also picks up shifts as a server in a local restaurant to help
pay the bills. She loves ministry work, but between all she is
juggling she finds her days dictated by her job or homework
demands. When those things aren't nagging her, the never-ending needs of ministry consume whatever time she has left. Tired
and stressed out describe how she feels most of the time. Seeing
others in her class successfully juggle similar demands makes her
feel like a failure. Reflecting on her private devotional life feels
like an additional burden to bear. When she stops to think about
it, she gets stuck in figuring out what to change, and she is beginning to lose a sense of purpose.

Most people can empathize with Sarah to some degree. You
may feel like you need a plan, but planning can feel like just
one more thing to do. God doesn't leave you without direction
in life. He is a God of plans. His nature regarding planning can
serve to guide you to live a life of purpose. Scripture reveals to us
God's character of intentional planning (Jeremiah 29:29). What

God has prepared will come to pass (Job 42:2; Isaiah 42:2; John 14:3). Psalm 33:11 tells us that the plans of the Lord stand firm. What is to be learned from this understanding that God is a God who plans? As an image bearer you should seek to mirror what you see in God in your own life. But before you rush to purchase an expensive planner, consider that God's planning is directly related to purposes. His plans are his purposes. As a believer, your life should align more and more with his purposes. Your plans should reflect his purposes.

Not everyone engages in planning to the same level. Some people set organized goals on a daily basis, while others only do so when they have something specific to plan for. This week you will take time to explore planning as a part of caring for yourself. Setting goals and mapping out direction allow you to live a more intentional life. There will always be curveballs, but having short-term plans or goals can keep you from living the overwhelmed life Sarah was experiencing.

Big goals have their place, but this week we are going to look at short-term goals. When you take time to make goals, be sure to keep in mind God's purpose for you. You have been called to a great commission (Matthew 28:19). Does your planning reflect that?

Setting short-term goals will help you feel less overwhelmed by your various responsibilities. In the same way a budget helps us steward the money we have been given, setting some realistic short-term goals is a way of stewarding the time we have been given. If you begin to accomplish small goals, you will be more inspired for the days ahead and may even find you have a fresh sense of purpose.

GOSPEL SPOTLIGHT

Our lives as Christians are ordered by a sovereign God who loved us enough to give his only Son for us. Remembering that he secured our eternal good helps us to live with purpose as we trust him in our day-to-day planning.

ACTION AND APPLICATION

Spiritual: Read the Scriptures referenced in this week's reading. Take some time to pray and meditate on what goals and plans God may have for you.

Emotional: Allowing emotions to dictate if and when we make plans is not a good idea. As you think about setting short-term goals, notice how you are emotionally reacting. Bullet journal all the feelings you notice when you think of setting goals or planning.

Physical: Sometimes physical surroundings affect our ability to meet goals. Clutter, disorganized workspaces, or unfinished projects can be distracting. Look around your house, desk, or workspace and address physical distractions you find.

Relational: Close friends and family members who know us well can be a source of help when assessing how to set realistic goals. After doing the goal-setting exercise below, share it with a friend or family member for feedback.

GUIDED JOURNALING

Choose one area of your life where you feel planning or goal setting could help to bring more purpose and clarity. It could be related to your work, ministry, spiritual life, relationships, or your daily routine. Start with only one area. Use the acronym SMART to set some purposeful goals for that area of your life.[9] Write your SMART goal in the space below.

- **S**pecific: What do I want to accomplish in one area of life at this time?
- **M**easurable: How will I know when I achieve my goal?

- Achievable: Is the goal attainable in light of my current resources and capacity?
- Realistic: How relevant is my goal to where God has me in life? How will this goal fit in with my current roles and responsibilities?
- Timely: What is a clear and reasonable time line for starting and finishing my goal?

WEEK 21
DO MORE BY DOING LESS

Most of us spend too much time on what is urgent, and not
enough time on what is important.

Stephen Covey

Long-distance runners know the importance of pacing. To
pace yourself simply means to monitor and adjust your speed
throughout the course of a race. Pacing has several purposes.
First, it ensures your ability to finish long races, because if you
start too fast, you might lose steam and never make it to the
finish line. Pacing is also a strategy for finishing the race as fast as
your personal capabilities allow.

Running coaches give specific suggestions when it comes to
pacing. In the case of a marathon, coaches suggest running the
first few miles at a slower pace than your goal pace to give your
body a chance to warm up. After the first three or four miles, you
speed up to your goal pace, and then for the final miles of the
race, you push hard and give everything you've got left. Starting
slower at the beginning allows marathon runners to finish faster
than if they had crossed the starting line at an overeager sprint.

This concept of pacing is helpful to consider within the context of self-care. When you are in the middle of important work,
it can feel like scrambling toward short-term gains will help you
accomplish the most. It's easy to spend your days mindlessly
hustling without thought of the future. You plant a church or
start a new ministry position and try to implement too many

ideas right from the start. You pile leading a Bible study and directing the children's ministry on top of your new career as a nurse. You try to meet every single need that comes your way, even though you feel overwhelmed and stretched too thin. Like a novice runner, you eagerly sprint from the starting line, and too often, this leads to exhaustion and burnout.

Wanting to do more for the Lord can be a worthy goal (Romans 12:11; Galatians 6:10; Titus 3:14), but too often we approach productivity in service to God in the wrong way. If we want to faithfully serve people over the course of a lifetime, we will have to learn to pace ourselves. To determine a pace that matches your personal capabilities, ask yourself if you would be able to sustain your lifestyle over the next decade. If not, something will need to change at some point. Often, change happens through slowing down, focusing on priorities, and cutting out extraneous activity. We will discuss how to work through this prioritizing process in detail in Week 22.

A lifetime of productive service to others and to the Lord is a marathon, not a sprint. Sustained faithfulness that perseveres over time will help us abound more in the work of the Lord (1 Corinthians 15:58) than a brief sprint at the beginning of a long career that leaves us gasping for breath just as we start. Slowing down does not equal doing less. Sometimes slowing down in the short run helps us do more in the long run. You will be more productive over the next ten years if you are mindful of how much you do on a daily and weekly basis right now. Working longer and more difficult hours does not necessarily add up to more work done for the Lord. Slow down today, and you may get more done over the course of your lifetime.

GOSPEL SPOTLIGHT

The most important mission a human has ever accomplished was not rushed or frenzied. Jesus was unhurried and undistracted in his work and public ministry. At just the right time, he secured our eternity with God (Romans 5:6).

ACTION AND APPLICATION

Spiritual: Consider how slowing down to recharge might be an important way to increase your overall productivity in the work God has called you to.

Emotional: Anxiety is one important sign that your current pace might be unsustainable. Take time to assess how slowing down might alleviate anxiety regarding this week's schedule.

Physical: Assess how your current pace is impacting your body. How long do you anticipate your body will be able to keep up this pace?

Relational: Has someone in your life asked you to slow down? If so, take some time right now to trim one or two things this week. This step in admitting your capacity can help you serve more faithfully.

GUIDED JOURNALING

Use the SMART goal-setting strategy you learned last week to set a long-term goal.

- **Specific:** What do I want to accomplish in one area of life this year? In the next five years?
- **Measurable:** How will I know when I achieve my goal?
- **Achievable:** Is the goal attainable in light of my current resources and capacity?
- **Realistic:** How relevant is my goal to where God has me in life? How will this goal fit in with my current roles and responsibilities?
- **Timely:** What is a clear and reasonable time line for starting and finishing my goal?

Once you set your long-term goal, consider how your current pace of life is hindering the accomplishment of this goal.

WEEK 22
YOU CAN'T DO EVERYTHING

The sober truth is that we are made of dust, even if we do aspire
to the heavens.

Dallas Willard

The world is filled with so many exciting ways to spend our time,
and sometimes I (Esther) wish I could do it all. At one point, doing everything felt more possible, but over the years, my physical
capacity has lessened. The onset of chronic illness changed my
ability to fill life to the brim, and I now have to carefully choose
where I use my energy each day.

Even though you may not share similar physical limitations,
it's likely there are times when you want to add something to
your schedule but realize you can't or shouldn't. Perhaps over the
years you have taken on a variety of activities and now realize
your life is too full. It's easy to say yes too often and become
stretched too thin. It's easy to become pulled in so many directions that it feels impossible to do anything well. We have many
dreams and plans for our lives. The individual tasks we take on
are often good things, but in combination they can become too
much. We start to wear out.

One way we can steward the energy and abilities God has
given us is to consider our responsibilities and decide which ones
are most important. Figuring out our priorities and focusing our
time and attention on a handful of carefully identified areas of

life is an important self-care strategy that flows from an understanding of two biblical truths: (1) we are finite and limited
(Psalm 103:14); and (2) God calls us to do our work with all our
heart (Colossians 3:23). In light of our human limitations, there
are only so many responsibilities we can complete wholeheartedly without burning out.

People have various capacities that differ based on physical
stamina, emotional resilience, financial resources, family circumstances, social support, and other factors. No matter your
capacity, steward it well by taking inventory. Consider your roles
and responsibilities in various areas of life. Are you a parent,
spouse, or friend? Consider your unique work tasks or ministry responsibilities. Is life filled with school assignments, housework, church commitments, or social events? Are any of your
responsibilities getting only your second best? If so, how do you
see this impacting people?

Most of us would agree that it's important to prioritize well,
knowing that we can only complete so much. Often the hard
part is figuring out *what* to prioritize. For many people, it can
help to begin by prioritizing people over projects. From there,
consider what it would look like to prioritize tasks and responsibilities that can only be done by you. Finally, ask yourself what
you are good at and what gives you life. We often have to prioritize tasks we don't like because they need to get done, but it can
also be helpful to consider what you enjoy as you go through this
pruning process.

Periodically reassessing your schedule is beneficial for everyone. You will feel less frazzled and receive more enjoyment from
the tasks and people you choose to prioritize. Other people will
stop getting your leftovers, which helps them flourish. You can't
do it all—at least not well—but you *can* give the best of your
energy and attention to the most important people and tasks
God has placed in your life.

GOSPEL SPOTLIGHT

Scripture reminds us that our priority is to "seek first his kingdom and his righteousness" (Matthew 6:33). Jesus reminded the Pharisees that the kingdom of God was already in their midst (Luke 17:20). To seek God's kingdom is to seek Christ and join his redemptive work. This mindset is a great place to start as we prioritize our lives.

ACTION AND APPLICATION

Spiritual: Does the way you fill your schedule reflect the fact that God created you to be finite and limited? If not, what might you need to change or let go?

Emotional: The next time you feel like you have too much on your plate, notice and name your emotions. What emotion do you feel? How does that emotion affect your actions?

Physical: What physical signs or limitations remind you that you can't do everything? What physical strengths tempt you to believe your energy stores are unlimited?

Relational: Who or what in your life should be getting *more* of your attention and energy? Who or what in your life should be getting *less* of your attention and energy?

GUIDED JOURNALING

Write out a list of all your responsibilities in life. Think in terms of categories (e.g., "housework" not "doing the dishes," or "family finances," not "paying bills"). Which responsibilities should get your energy and attention first? What responsibilities, if any, do you need to cut out of your life to be able to wholeheartedly complete what is most important?

WEEK 23
SEEK RIGHTEOUS DESIRES

May he grant you your heart's desire and fulfill all your plans!

Psalm 20:4

What do you want in life? Many of us aren't used to considering this question because it seems like the wrong question to ask. As we are often reminded, God is more concerned with our holiness than our happiness. Fulfilling our desires in life is not the goal. I absolutely believe these statements are true. At the same time, I don't think we should ignore this question completely.

Considering our preferences is an important part of life planning. Too often, we overanalyze decisions about work, relationships, free time, and so many other areas of life. We become stuck as we try to figure out the exact right thing to do. "What is God's will for me in this area of life?" we wonder. This question is important, but God does not always give us a clear road map forward. Many times, the future offers a variety of options to choose from. Which job will we take next? How will we spend our Monday evenings? Will we stay single, get married, or have children? There isn't always one right option. In these situations, how do we decide?

As we set goals and make life decisions, sometimes the best way forward is to consider what we want. While certainly our desires can be deceitful and lead us astray (James 1:13–15), we should not conclude that all desires are wrong. As we search Scripture, we can determine those times when our desires align with God's will and God's law (Psalm 40:8). God can fulfill the desires of those who fear him (Psalm 145:19), because when we live in fear of God, we keep the good of others in mind and God's bigger story in view.

We should approach life planning with the goal of seeking first God's kingdom and his righteousness (Matthew 6:33). With this as our underlying mindset, we are free to make many big and small decisions based on our preferences. As long as we are seeking God and considering the needs of others, we can choose from the options available to us. Would you rather go into ministry, become an accountant, or work in construction? You get to choose. Do you want to run a marathon or take up canoeing as a hobby? You are free to do both. Would you rather spend your Monday evenings cultivating family time or going to a Bible study? Either could be a good option if you take the above mindset to heart.

Many times our plans do not succeed, and we often do not get what we want. When life does not go our way, this is an opportunity to submit to God's plans without letting anger or dissatisfaction take over. Sometimes God works through difficult divine interruptions, as we will talk about next week. These interruptions reveal those times when we are holding our plans as more important than God. This is an occasion to ask forgiveness and follow his best purpose for our lives. Other times, he grants our hearts' desires and fulfills all our plans (Psalm 20:4). When God allows us to work, play, and build relationships in the ways we prefer, these realized desires are "sweet to the soul" (Proverbs 13:19). They are good for our self-care. It is then our privilege to share the overflow of God's good gifts to us with our families, friends, and those we serve.

GOSPEL SPOTLIGHT

Jesus's ultimate desire was to do the will of his Father. His prayer as he anticipated the pain of the cross was, "not my will, but yours, be done" (Luke 22:42). The more we seek God, the more our desires align with his.

ACTION AND APPLICATION

Spiritual: Meditate on Proverbs 13:19 NASB: "Desire realized is sweet to the soul." Take some time to thank God for the kindness of desires realized.

Emotional: What is one good and holy desire that would make you feel happier and more fulfilled? If that desire aligns with God's law and does not negatively impact other people, pursue it this week.

Physical: What is a good and holy desire you have that would make life easier, better, or more comfortable physically? If that desire aligns with God's law and does not negatively impact other people, pursue it this week.

Relational: When you allow yourself to pursue your desires, how does this impact your family and other people? When you never allow yourself to pursue things you want, how does this impact them?

GUIDED JOURNALING

Psalm 37:4 says, "Delight yourself in the LORD, and he will give you the desires of your heart." Take a moment now and surrender any desires that keep you from delighting in the Lord. Journal starting with this sentence: Lord, I desire to live for you. Help me to seek you first by . . .

WEEK 24
DIVINE INTERRUPTION

Because God loves you, he will willingly interrupt or
compromise your momentary happiness in order to accomplish
one more step in the process of transformation.

Paul David Tripp

Has God ever interrupted your life with a forced pause? For me
(Esther) it was carpal tunnel and tendinitis in both hands and
wrists. As someone who spends all day working on my computer, this sudden interruption felt like the last thing I needed.
It felt unfair. I felt angry. Why would God interrupt my work
and life in this way? As the pain lingered and my time on the
computer diminished, I saw that God was pausing my life for a
reason. This interruption was not a punishment. God was using
it to grab my attention, to help me slow down, and to prompt
me to consider the direction of my life.

Inconvenient interruptions snap us out of tunnel vision.
Many times, we charge ahead in life without pausing to periodically reassess in which direction we are headed. We function on
autopilot in relation to our work, ministry, family, and how we
spend our time in general. For months or even years, we don't
stop to consider what might need to change. We don't slow down
enough to ask if we are living out the purpose God has for us.

Has God recently interrupted your life? Has he forced you
to slow down in frustrating ways? Are you facing closed doors

that don't make sense? Has God blocked your ministry, work, or forward progress? Interruptions like these can be confusing. While they are happening, it often feels like they are keeping us from the real work God has for us to do. In reality, God often uses forced pauses to get our attention and redirect us toward *his* purpose for us. As Proverbs 19:21 reminds us, "Many are the plans in the mind of a man, but it is the purpose of the LORD that will stand."

What does all of this have to do with self-care? As you figure out what God is doing, use times of pause to focus on caring for yourself in preparation for what comes next. This season may *feel* like wasted time, but see it as an opportunity to draw near to God, strengthen your body, attend to your mind, and focus on your relationships. Healing happens when we slow down. Growth occurs when we resist the temptation to doubt God and lean into trusting him instead. Spiritual refreshment comes when we seek God first even when life doesn't make sense.

God's purpose in your life *will* prevail. As you face interruptions, pay close attention. This could be a good time to consider your future. Take some time to assess the plans in your heart and see if they seem to be in line with the purpose of God. Spend some time in prayer and ask yourself if God is asking you to make any changes. Use divine interruptions as an opportunity to take needed care for yourself so that, when circumstances change, you can be better prepared for what God has for you.

GOSPEL SPOTLIGHT

Consider the interruption Jesus experienced when he chose to leave heaven, become human, suffer, and die. When interruptions and suffering seem to block your plans for the future, remember how God's good plan for humanity was fulfilled through the suffering of Christ.

ACTION AND APPLICATION

Spiritual: When life is interrupted, take note of what it leads you to believe about God. Are the thoughts and beliefs you have about him true?

Emotional: Interruptions can bring up a number of negative emotions. Practice looking at your emotions before judging them or trying to get rid of them. What are you feeling right now? Are you tempted to push that feeling away? Try approaching that emotion and bringing it to God instead of distancing yourself from it.

Physical: Is a physical limitation keeping you from doing all that you want to do right now? It doesn't have to be a major physical issue. For example, maybe it is headaches, trouble sleeping, digestive issues, muscle pain, or injury. How can you use times of physical limitation to focus on being with God in ways you often don't when these limitations are not present?

Relational: Use times of interruption to reevaluate the direction of your family or other relationships. Set some new priorities together. Discuss what purpose God might have for you right now.

GUIDED JOURNALING

Has God recently interrupted your life? How might this interruption be an opportunity to reassess your life, make changes, or focus on preparing your whole self for whatever God might have for you next? Write out what changes first come to your mind as you answer these questions.

WEEK 25
SCREENLESS OR LESS SCREENS?

> The answer to our hyperkinetic digital world of diversions is the soul-calming sedative of Christ's splendor, beheld with the mind and enjoyed by the soul.
>
> *Tony Reinke*

Have you experienced screen fatigue? Of course you have. Burning, tired eyes coupled with blurred vision. A dull headache. Brain fog. Neck and shoulder tension. Exhaustion. We all know the symptoms. In fact, we know them too well. Yet screens still captivate us. For most people, screens are the first thing reached for in the day and the last thing held at night. Unhealthy screen habits may be the most embraced and acceptable vices of all time.

I (Eliza) am guilty of poor screen habits, and I have often experienced screen fatigue. Yes, me, the author of a book on screen use. I'm not immune to the pull. In fact, I wrote *Raising Kids in a Screen-Saturated World* partially out of the personal challenges I faced as I raised my children. In spite of these downsides, the good that screens bring to life is tremendous. I don't think life would be better without them. The convenience and connection they provide afford benefits too numerous to name. Biblical self-care includes an understanding of how screens should be used (or not used) for the glory of God.

In the first part of Isaiah 43, we are given a moving picture of how the Lord feels about his people. His children are described as precious, honored, and loved. He emphasizes how valuable they are as shown by the wealth he willingly exchanges for them. He confirms his unfailing commitment to them in the repeated reminders of his presence with them as they go through difficult times. Take a moment and read Isaiah 43:1–7.

Before you wonder if I just changed the subject, let's return to verse 7 and carefully notice what the words say. The verse describes God's people as, "everyone who is called by my name, *whom I created for my glory*, whom I formed and made" (emphasis added). We, God's children, were created to live our lives for God's glory.

How do we live for God's glory? We could look for a manual, or we can look for a model. God gave us both. Scripture is the manual. And the model? The perfect model of a life lived for God's glory is Jesus. God intends us to live like Jesus, and that includes how we use screens. "Well," you say, "the last time I looked, Jesus didn't have any screens, so does that mean I shouldn't either?" Screens or no screens is not what it means to live like Jesus. Living like Jesus means following his example in prioritizing life. He was a busy man and had many things that could have fully occupied him. He lived a balanced life that had his father's will and work as the object of his continual attention. We must apply his example to how we use screens.

Without intentional efforts, screens will dominate our lives in unhealthy ways. We can use screens to the glory of God by setting parameters to guard against the pull of the scroll. Limiting the use of social media, websites, and apps that draw us in and absorb our time can be helpful. Creating rhythms that incorporate non-screen engagement with God such as the meditation described in Week 4 or slowing down which we will look at in Week 26 help us to guard against the distractions of screens. Utilizing digital wellness tools on devices to shut off or limit nonessential screen use provides accountability. All these strategies create space to engage in undistracted time with God and others.

Our bodies tell us when we need a break. We all know the signs. We may not need to go screenless in order to rest in a digital age. Instead we may need to consider how we can use our screens less. This will mean using our screens in intentional ways that are more conducive to rest, health, wellness, and the glory of God.

GOSPEL SPOTLIGHT

If your screen habits reveal ways you have veered from honoring the Lord or you know your use of screens does not bring glory to God, take a moment to confess this. In Jesus, you are fully forgiven.

ACTION AND APPLICATION

Spiritual: Honestly assess how screens have impacted your spiritual life. Do they enhance or diminish your focused time of prayer or Bible reading? This week don't use your phone to read the Bible. Have your prayer time away from any screen. Notice any difference.

Emotional: Screens can be used as an emotional anesthesia. The next time you experience a difficult emotion (anger, sadness, loneliness, boredom, et cetera) avoid turning to a screen. Instead talk to someone about how you are feeling or journal your thoughts with a pen and paper.

Physical: Screens promote a sedentary life. Look for ways this week to replace nonessential screen time with physical activity. Take a walk, stretch, exercise, or move to your favorite music instead of mindlessly scrolling.

Relational: What relationship is most impacted by your screen use? Prioritize keeping your phone out of sight, or your TV or laptop off, and spend intentional time with that person this week.

GUIDED JOURNALING

Make a list of the positive and negative ways you use screens in your life. As you review the list, consider ways you can glorify God with your screen use. Where do you need to make changes?

WEEK 26
SLOW DOWN AND CONSIDER

Build into your life unhurried quiet . . .

Dane Ortlund

Matthew 6:25–30 is best known as a passage that addresses how to deal with anxiety. The passage reminds us that if God takes care of the birds and the flowers, we can be assured he will take care of us as well. The promise brings hope and calm to an anxious heart. But the passage holds another lesson. In taking the time to stop and observe the birds and the flowers, we learn to live life at a slower pace—a pace that takes the time to observe and enjoy the amazing creativity of God.

Our lives are often lived at an exhausting speed. Because of this we don't often take time to consider things. Matthew 6:28 tells us to "consider the lilies." Here, "consider" means "to learn thoroughly" or "examine carefully."[10] To consider something takes time. A modern-day translation of "consider the lilies" would be "stop and smell the roses." Take the time to slow down and enjoy what God has created. The passage also tells us to look at the birds. It doesn't say glance or take a quick peek. This is more of a fixed gaze than a glimpse. This passage is telling us to be unhurried when it comes to looking at creation because the lessons there are important and learned slowly.

I (Eliza) have always loved the outdoors. Perhaps being born in a cabin deep in the northern forest of Montana set a course for this love. Or maybe it was the many hikes and camping trips my mother took us on as children. Or maybe, and probably more likely, it is the wonder found in nature that teaches me about my God. Seeing the detailed folds on a single flower petal or the kaleidoscope of color on the eyes of a tiny insect excites me with how gloriously detailed God is in creation.

This morning as I took a walk outdoors along a nearby trail, I caught sight of a dark shape on the underside of a low-lying leaf. As I approached it, I saw it was a black swallowtail butterfly only minutes old, drying its wings. Still gripping its empty chrysalis, the butterfly was hanging upside down, resting from its recent release. The details of that little creation captivated me. Several runners, mountain bikers, and hikers passed me on the trail as I watched the young insect slowly fan its wings, giving me a slow-motion view of its majesty. No one stopped to ask what I was looking at. They all seemed to have their own purpose for being on the trail that did not include stopping to look at a newborn butterfly. I took out my phone and took several pictures for my social media friends who, whether they want to or not, get to see all my trail finds. Before I left this now sacred spot, I uttered the words I often do when I see something like that: "Thank you!"

This moment of slowing down to consider God's creation reminded me that God wants us to be dazzled by him. He has given us endless displays of his creative glory. Slowing down enough just to look at the beautiful painted canvas of the butterfly's wings, I was astounded by the detail the Lord takes in creating. I worshiped at that tree and left there more excited about being a child of God than when I first encountered the black shadow under the tree leaf. I was reminded of the care that God takes in creation, and that reminder made the weight of my bustling life a little lighter. I left with more gratitude in my heart than when I had set out on the trail that morning.

Dane Ortlund, in *Gentle and Lowly*, asks an important question: "Why not build into your life unhurried quiet, where, among other disciplines, you consider the radiance of who he actually is, what animates him, what his deepest delight is? Why not give your soul room to be enchanted with Christ time and again?"[11] That little black-winged butterfly did just that, and my soul was warmed toward our shared Creator. But it took being unhurried. I had to consider, to look, to behold. This week, make space for a deep look at the birds, the flowers, or maybe even the butterflies.

GOSPEL SPOTLIGHT

One of the most amazing things God does is to make people into new creations. Think back to when you first came to know Jesus. Remember the joy you had of knowing you belonged to God. Take time to consider anew the wonder of your salvation. If you have not personally experienced new life with Christ, we invite you to pray a simple prayer of repentance and faith asking God to save you. Share this decision with a Christian you look up to.

ACTION AND APPLICATION

Spiritual: When was the last time you allowed creation to revive your soul? This week, notice the trees, the birds, or flowers you see outside. Consider what you see as encounters with God.

Emotional: Take some time right now and list things in creation that stir your emotions toward God.

Physical: Being outside has therapeutic and restorative effects on our bodies. If possible, take a walk every day this week. If you are unable to walk, try sitting outside for ten minutes and listen and notice all that is around you. Even if you live in a busy city, notice the beauty of the sky, the grass, or a gentle breeze.

Relational: Consider how your pace of life has impacted your relationships. Pray and ask the Lord to show you how to bring others into some unhurried time outside this week.

GUIDED JOURNALING

Write about the last time creation stirred your soul. Use as much detail as possible.

SECTION 4
COMMUNITY LIFE

WEEK 27
LIVING AS ONE BODY

Believers are never told to become one; we already are one and
are expected to act like it.

Joni Eareckson Tada

Independence is in our DNA. Despite the fact that we were designed to need God and others, we still buy into the thinking
that we can manage on our own. Even though the Bible calls us
one body, believers live with an independent mindset, down-
playing the biblical reality that we need one another. This is contrary to what the Bible says about how we ought to live. We are
one body with many members, and we need each other. It was
God's design that we help and support one another.

As I (Eliza) write this I am recovering from a pulled muscle.
Apparently, we have over 650 muscles in our bodies, but right
now this one muscle is getting a lot of my attention. It hurts at
the source, but the rest of my body feels it as well. I cannot walk
as I normally would, and since the muscle is in my back, I feel
the muscle with every breath I take. One pulled muscle affects
my whole body, and my whole body must cooperate in the re-
covery process. I need the strong parts of the body to support
this weakened part.

When one part of your physical body has a need, you know
about it. You give it the necessary attention. The rest of your body
accommodates willingly to help and support the part of your
body that has need. How strikingly similar this physical response

is to how the body of Christ is encouraged to serve one another. In 1 Corinthians 12:12–27, we are given important direction on this reality. Take a moment right now and read the passage slowly. We are encouraged to see the value of our brothers and sisters in Christ and to care for one another. Toward the end of that passage we see this truth: "If one member suffers, all suffer together; if one member is honored, all rejoice together" (v. 26).

This passage highlights a distinctive difference between how the world views self-care and how the body of Christ views it. Secular self-care centers on you meeting your own needs. You might hire someone to help meet your needs, but they often have little to no relationship with you beyond your specific need. They may help you toward health or wellness—they may come alongside you and take on some of your responsibilities—but they do not fully enter your struggle or carry it with you. The body of believers is different. Christian community is necessary in biblical self-care. Being one body, we must embrace the truth that when we struggle, others struggle with us. Our need for care calls other believers to action. It also means that when others are in need we are invested in their care. We willingly participate in, encourage, and support measures that bring health to the *members* of the body of believers, knowing how vitally connected we all are.

Living as one body means encouraging others to participate in self-care. Affirm your brother or sister when they make decisions to care for their emotional and physical health. Support their efforts to attend to their needs. This may mean watching little ones so a mom can get some rest. It could look like providing a meal for a weary family, or maybe it means sharing the resources God has blessed you with. And, as we will see in future weeks, it also looks like inviting others to help you care for yourself. This reciprocal involvement in one another's self-care results in health and well-being for the body of believers. Everyone flourishes when we depend on and support one another.

GOSPEL SPOTLIGHT

The picture of *one body* in Scripture illustrates our salvation. As believers, we have been made a part of Christ's body. We are forever united together by the work of Jesus to serve and help one another (1 Corinthians 12:27).

ACTION AND APPLICATION

Spiritual: How are other believers caring for your soul? Is there an area of your spiritual life that needs attention right now? Consider sharing your needs with a brother or sister and ask them for help or prayer.

Emotional: Vulnerability is a key component to sharing your need for self-care. Identify any emotional discomfort you feel as you think about revealing your needs to others. In humility, share your needs with someone you trust.

Physical: We often wait until there are no other options before we ask for help from other believers. This week consider one area of physical need that you can share with a brother or sister in Christ. Take the step to ask for their help.

Relational: Think of one person you can help encourage or support in their efforts to care for themselves this week. Write their name here _____. Think of one person you can ask to help you care for yourself this week. Write their name here _____.

GUIDED JOURNALING

When we share our need for personal care with others, we are often asked the question: "How can I help?" This is a question we are not well prepared to answer. Do a bullet journal exercise of ways others can support and help you in caring for yourself. Refer to this list when someone asks how they can help you. For directions on how to bullet journal see the appendix.

WEEK 28
THE HEALING NATURE OF
CONVERSATION

Kind words can be short and easy to speak, but their echoes are truly endless.

Mother Teresa

At first glance, conversation might not seem like a means of self-care. Upon closer reflection, I (Esther) realize that the regular conversations I have with family members and friends top my list of ways I care for myself. Daily texts and videos with sisters and close friends. Reflecting on the day each evening with my husband. Occasional coffee dates with a friend. Small talk after church. Sharing and listening in the context of ordinary conversations encourages me in ways I don't find anywhere else.

I recently left a coffee date with a friend feeling lighter than I had in days. A sense of peace, contentment, and happiness filled my soul. This friend listens well. She asks good questions and freely shares about her life. One of her gifts is an ability to bring conversations back to Jesus in a natural way. I left the coffee shop feeling less alone, more understood, and more grounded in my faith.

The book of Proverbs helped make sense of my experience that day. Throughout Proverbs, we learn that words have immense power. They have great potential to heal and great capacity to harm. Proverbs 12:18 says, "There is one whose rash words are like sword thrusts, but the tongue of the wise brings healing."

Words can be especially healing when they lead us to remember what Jesus has to say about the struggles we face. As I talked with my friend in the coffee shop, she reminded me of the grace and freedom I have in Christ. This was good news I needed to hear, and she helped me hear it in a way that connected with what I was facing right at that moment.

At the same time, our conversations do not always need to be deep or spiritual to be healing. Sometimes we simply need words that are gentle (Proverbs 15:4) or glad (Proverbs 12:25). Small talk, connecting through humor, and sharing about the events of our day are all important ways we receive care and give care to others.

Sometimes conversations like this feel out of reach. I have not always had friendships like this in my life. Not everyone has family members who offer kind words. Living alone can make regular healing conversations hard to find. Our schedules fill up, leaving little time or energy for meaningful conversation. What should we do when we long for healing conversations but aren't sure where to find them?

Experiencing healing conversations often begins when we speak healing words into other people's lives. Consider what this might look like with each person you encounter this week. It could be a family member, friend, coworker, or stranger. As you enter conversations, ask yourself a few questions. What gentle, glad, or encouraging word can I offer? What humorous anecdote about my day might help me make a new connection or bring joy into someone's life? What gospel encouragement or wise counsel might be welcomed in this moment? As we intentionally initiate conversations that are healing to others, we often find that people respond in kind.

GOSPEL SPOTLIGHT

Our ultimate healing comes not from the words of people, but from the Word of God (Psalm 107:20) through Christ Jesus (John 1:14).

ACTION AND APPLICATION

Spiritual: How has your faith been strengthened through the conversations you had this week? Which people in your life tend to strengthen your faith through their words?

Emotional: Think of someone you enjoy talking to. How does this person make you feel as you engage in conversation with them?

Physical: Proverbs 16:24 NIV says, "Gracious words are a honeycomb, sweet to the soul and healing to the bones." In what ways have you experienced health in your body as a result of pleasant conversations?

Relational: If you experience a lack of healing conversation in your life, start by considering how you can speak healing words into other people's lives. Think of one person who you know needs encouragement. When and where will you plan to speak healing words into their life?

GUIDED JOURNALING

Keep track of the healing conversations you have this week. Note when you have the opportunity to speak healing words into other people's lives. Pay attention to those times when other people bless you through conversation. Journal about what you learn about God, yourself, others, and self-care as you are intentional in the way you enter conversations.

WEEK 29
ASK FOR WHAT YOU NEED

> Nourishment is always far more than biological nutrition. We
> are nourished by our communities.
>
> *Tish Harrison Warren*

Desperate and depleted, John sat down across from his counselor. Between caring for his aging parents and managing crisis after crisis at work, he had been running on empty for a long time. So many people and projects relied on him and his ability to function, so he buckled down and kept going. A few months earlier, he realized a breakdown might be imminent. He cut out as many commitments as he could, but even this was not enough. He kept going and pretended everything was fine, because he didn't want to burden people with his problems. He hoped he would eventually make it through to the other side on his own.

The other side never came, and the breakdown was worse than he imagined. One night he woke up in a state of distress. His heart raced out of his chest, he couldn't breathe, and he felt like he was going to die. The next morning, a doctor informed him he had experienced a panic attack. Desperate for relief, John scheduled a counseling appointment to try and make sense of what went wrong.

John's experience represents a common scenario. Even after properly aligning priorities and cutting out unnecessary commitments, some people find themselves in a place where they do not have enough physical, mental, spiritual, financial, or other resources to meet all of their responsibilities on their own. Instead of asking for help, they trudge forward, too ashamed to admit they are not doing well. The last thing they want to do is bother people with their problems.

It's easy to fall into the mindset that it is somehow disgraceful to need help, but limited resources are not something to feel ashamed about. Everything we have comes from God (1 Chronicles 29:14), and it is possible to steward well all the resources he has given us and still not have enough to meet our daily needs and responsibilities on our own. Certain life circumstances can quickly leave us functioning with a resource deficit. Health problems, caretaking responsibilities, recent losses, difficult relationships, and stressful jobs are a few examples. In situations such as these, we are sometimes forced to use tomorrow's resources today, and this is not the way God intends for us to live.

When we find ourselves in this place, it's better for everyone if we ask our community to step in to help carry what we cannot (Galatians 6:2). It is God's design for us to care for each other in community. The work he has called us to is not meant to be done alone. What help do you need right now? Have you avoided telling people about your need? Have you refused assistance when asked? What if you asked someone for help with childcare or accepted that offer for a meal? Do you need help with yard work, or would it make sense to ask your church to help pay for counseling? This week, consider what you might need from your community.

Whatever it is, don't be afraid to ask. Asking for help not only guards our health and sanity when life is falling part but it's also important for the health of our souls. It reminds us of the reality of our human nature. We cannot save ourselves. We cannot do life on our own. God does not ask us to have it all together. Quite the contrary, he invites us to admit our weakness, confess our sin, and receive his strength and salvation. He invites us to acknowledge our insufficiencies and allow others to carry our burdens with us.

GOSPEL SPOTLIGHT

Matthew 25:34–46 teaches that whenever you offer help to those in need, it is as though you are offering help to Jesus. Have you ever considered this in reverse? The care people offer you is being offered to Jesus as well. For this they will receive earthly blessing and eternal reward.

ACTION AND APPLICATION

Spiritual: Do you find it hard to admit when you need help? Identify what happens in your heart when you are forced to reckon with areas of weakness and limitation.

Emotional: What emotional or mental burdens, if any, are you struggling with that others in your community may be able to help you carry? Write what comes to mind.

Physical: Sometimes the first signs of needing help show up in the form of physical symptoms. In what ways, if any, is your body signaling the need to ask for help?

Relational: It's easy to wait for a crisis to occur before asking for help. Try breaking that pattern this week. Write down the name of one trustworthy person in your life. Schedule a time to talk with that person about any struggles you are going through and how you can support each other.

GUIDED JOURNALING

Journal through this prompt.
God, I feel weak and needy in . . .
I need my community to help me with . . .
This need reminds me just how much I must trust you for . . .

WEEK 30
MIRRORING GOD'S
GENEROUS CREATIVITY

[God] must've had a blast. Painting the stripes on the zebra,
hanging the stars in the sky, putting the gold in the sunset. . . . And
then, as a finale to a brilliant performance, he made . . . a human
who had the unique honor to bear the stamp, "In His Image."

Max Lucado

My friend, Christine, and I (Esther) like to talk about our dogs.
One day as we discussed their latest antics, I confessed that I
sometimes feel guilty about owning two enormous dogs who
eat expensive food and run up expensive vet bills. Wouldn't our
money be better spent somewhere else? My friend's response was
thoughtful. "It's incredible to me that God created these wild animals that now roam through our houses and keep us company.
God created them for us. They are for our enjoyment!"

I have to agree with her assessment. God was generous to
include them in creation and give them to us as companions.
Underneath the surface, my dogs are wild animals that stand
watch at our front window, barking ferociously at passersby. This
is their territory—trespassers beware. At the end of the day, they
are goofy fur babies who just want to be fed and loved. They
have personalities and quirks. They cuddle and keep us company. They bring immense joy into our lives, and I am thankful
God included them in creation.

"In the beginning, God created" (Genesis 1:1). The very first thing we learn about God's character is that he is our Creator. Looking at what he has made, we see he often had our enjoyment in mind. Goofy and ferocious dogs. Brilliant sunsets and calming forests. Ocean breezes and delicious foods for savoring. God's creation is artistic and original, inventive and unexpected. All created for us. God's final act of creation was man, a creature created in his own image (Genesis 2:26). After creating Adam, God included him in the creative process, giving Adam the job of naming all of the animals (Genesis 3:19–20). God the Creator— mankind the creation made to mirror the creative nature of God.

God brings new and good things into the world, and he invites us to join in that process. Some of us are more naturally creative than others. While some people can't help but be drawn into creative endeavors, others don't practice creativity because they feel they are not good at it. Still other people don't take time for creative passions because they consciously or subconsciously believe that "practical" types of work are more worthwhile. No matter our natural tendencies, we all can use a reminder that we mirror God's character when we create things that bless others.

When we write poetry, sing music, cook on the grill, plant gardens, decorate a room, or use our hands to build, we bring new and good things into the world that fill people with joy and other pleasing emotions. If God has given you untapped creative talents, use them! God's creation reminds us that life is not all about practicalities. If creating is the air you breathe, be more intentional about using your talents in ways that bring enjoyment into the lives of others. Like so many other areas of self-care, creativity is not just for the good it brings into our lives, but for the ways it blesses others.

GOSPEL SPOTLIGHT
Because of Christ's work on the cross, the whole world will one day be restored. Creating things can be an act of restoration and

redemption that mirrors the transformational work Christ has done and will do for all of creation.

ACTION AND APPLICATION

Spiritual: Acts of creativity reflect God's nature. If you are someone who doesn't take time for creative passions, how might this give you permission to spend more time and energy on this area of life?

Emotional: Our emotions can be expressed through creativity. Think of a time when you felt happy or at peace. Write a poem, song, or article about this experience. If this is new for you, give yourself plenty of grace. It does not have to be perfect.

Physical: Use your hands to create something good and new this week. Paint a picture. Build something for your house. Bake a cake. Decorate a room with beautiful colors. Start a garden. If you already tend to spend a lot of time creating, try a new modality that you don't normally use.

Relational: Use your creativity to bless someone this week. What type of creative activity will you choose? Who will you share your creation with?

GUIDED JOURNALING

Our creative skills come from God (Exodus 35:35). Journal about some of the creative skills God has given you. How can you be more intentional about using these skills to bring other people enjoyment?

WEEK 31
CELEBRATE LIKE JESUS

God is trying to call us back to that for which He created us, to worship Him and to enjoy Him forever.

A. W. Tozer

You might say there are two types of people in the world—people who need a reminder that Jesus wept (John 11:35) and people who need a reminder that Jesus celebrated (Luke 5:29). I (Esther) definitely fall into the second category. Acknowledging grief comes naturally to me. Celebrating is another story. Somewhere along the way, I absorbed a feeling that work is important and parties can wait. Who has time to celebrate when life is so busy? Who *wants* to celebrate when life is so difficult?

Are you good at celebrating? If you tend to live on the lighter side of life, this may seem like a strange question. It may surprise you that celebration does not come naturally for some people. People who struggle to celebrate are missing out on an important means of self-care because caring for ourselves requires balance. Rest, work, play, and celebration rejuvenate us in different ways and provide different opportunities for us to care for others. No matter your natural leaning, our propensities can serve each other. I need my friends who know how to throw parties. Perhaps you need friends who know how to weep. Jesus was good at both. His life provides several examples of how we might approach celebration in our own lives.

Jesus celebrated life's happy moments by attending parties. On one occasion, Jesus and his disciples were invited to a wedding (see John 2:1–11). He did not turn down the invitation to spend time on something "more important." Not only did he attend the wedding, but when the wine ran out, he also chose to perform his first public miracle. At the prompting of his mother, he turned jars of water into high-quality wine, and we can imagine this wine may have fueled the party late into the night. Jesus could have chosen to have his first miracle take place in response to suffering. He did eventually show his divine nature in those moments as well, but he chose a celebration to be the first place he revealed his glory to the world (John 2:11).

Jesus also attended parties to build relationships with unexpected people. After being called to follow Jesus, Levi organized a great feast for him that was also attended by a crowd of tax collectors and sinners (Luke 5:29). When the Pharisees saw this, they were incensed. Why would Jesus party with such questionable company? Jesus's answer revealed his mission: "It is not the healthy who need a doctor, but the sick. I have not come to call the righteous, but sinners to repentance" (Luke 5:31–32 NIV). Festivities break down barriers, and Jesus used this feast as an opportunity to connect with people who needed his message.

Perhaps celebration does not come naturally to you. Or, maybe you tend to use celebration in unhealthy ways. Jesus's example can help us all. When was the last time you attended a party as a way to connect with people and build relationships? Do you ever use celebration as a way to rejuvenate yourself physically or give yourself a mental break? Look over your schedule and note the last time you paused to celebrate a happy moment. Perhaps this week would be a good time to add a few intentional celebrations to this year's calendar.

GOSPEL SPOTLIGHT

Jesus first revealed his glory at a celebration, and an even greater celebration of his glory waits for us in heaven (Revelation 19:7). For now, our singing and worshiping, rejoicing and feasting, dancing and celebrating is only a foretaste of what is to come.

ACTION AND APPLICATION

Spiritual: Jesus celebrated. Do you take time to celebrate as he did?

Emotional: Sum up your emotional reaction to celebratory events. For example, do they fill you with joy or discomfort? Excitement or exhaustion? Anticipation or guilt?

Physical: Sometimes pausing from work to celebrate can be physically rejuvenating. Other times, celebration harms our bodies through overindulgence in unhealthy foods and alcohol. Notice how celebration tends to impact your body and consider any needed changes.

Relational: Jesus's life teaches us that parties are an opportunity to connect with people for the mere joy of celebrating happy moments and for the purpose of sharing your faith. Plan a celebration! What will you celebrate? Who will you invite to celebrate with you?

GUIDED JOURNALING

Journal through any barriers that stop you from celebrating. What steps will you take to remove these barriers? How does your celebration here on earth demonstrate to others that you believe the best is yet to come?

WEEK 32
ENTERTAINMENT FOR SELF-CARE?

Only what God has commanded in His word should be
regarded as binding; in all else there may be liberty of actions.

John Owen

A book on self-care would not be complete without a discussion on
entertainment. Entertainment can easily turn addictive and self-indulgent and *impede* our self-care. When used wisely and in healthy
and moderate ways it can *assist* our self-care. Whether it comes in
the form of watching TV in the evenings to unwind, playing video
games on the weekends for enjoyment, singing out loud to your
favorite music to let loose, or scrolling through silly videos on social
media for a laugh, entertainment is a huge part of people's lives.

Entertainment has both benefits and pitfalls. When it comes
to the topic of entertainment, Christians should approach it with
the mindset of liberty and love for neighbor. We are free to make
unique and different choices regarding the forms of entertainment we participate in. In fact, we, the authors, each have a different, almost opposite, approach to entertainment. Our individual approaches are influenced by various factors like our family
lives, personal preferences, and life circumstances. One thing we
agree on is that our entertainment choices should not be hurtful
to others or cause us to neglect our neighbor. Rather, our entertainment choices should enrich our lives and the lives of others.

While certain guidelines apply to all, what we don't want to
do is to provide a step-by-step approach for how everyone should

engage entertainment. Instead, we want to spark some thoughts to help you assess your own approach to it. This entry is a little bit different than the others. Unlike previous weeks, we are going to ask more questions and encourage you to do a bit more of the work. One uncompromising commitment is that entertainment choices should never indulge sin. Having that laid out, we encourage you to consider matters of conscience and underlying motives as guidelines for what entertainment you choose to engage.

To help you assess this area of life, we offer one passage of Scripture to guide you: "And you shall love the Lord your God with all your heart and with all your soul and with all your mind and with all your strength. . . . [and] You shall love your neighbor as yourself" (Mark 12:30–31). This week consider how this command to love God and others governs your entertainment choices.

Your Heart: Does the content of your entertainment convict your conscience? Does the form of your entertainment soften your heart toward the Spirit's work in your life?

Your Soul: Is your entertainment causing you to engage in sinful pleasures? Does your entertainment invigorate your love for God and his good gifts?

Your Mind: Has entertainment turned into addiction? Does it lead to mental exhaustion, sleepless nights, distractedness, and obsessive behaviors? Do you feel like your time spent in entertainment gives you mental refreshment or reset?

Your Strength: How does your body feel after you use entertainment? Does your approach promote laziness and enable avoidance of healthy levels of activity? Or, does entertainment help you to rest or strengthen your body?

Your Neighbor: Has extended entertainment time led you to neglect important people in your life? Do you tend to use entertainment to isolate? Or, do you seek to use entertainment in community to enhance connection with family and friends?

We hope that as you examine your entertainment through the lens of this passage you feel the freedom to engage and enjoy those things that align with this great commandment (Mark 12:30–31). With that in mind, embrace what brings enjoyment to life as a means of taking care of yourself.

GOSPEL SPOTLIGHT

Entertainment is another area where believers have freedom in Christ. Entertainment choices should not be grounded in legalistic attempts to govern behavior. Instead, our choices are opportunities to use our freedom for the purpose of loving others the way Jesus sacrificially loved us.

ACTION AND APPLICATION

Spiritual: Examine your conscience. Pray for discernment in your media and entertainment choices. Does your entertainment create distance between you and God?

Emotional: Seek out one form of entertainment this week that evokes positive feelings toward God. Listen to a song that leads to grateful praise. Watch a documentary that compels you to feel wonder at the great work he has done. Find an award-winning movie that brings you joy or excitement as you observe the common good he has given to all through creative talents.

Physical: Choose one form of entertainment you would normally do on a screen and do it off-line or in person this week instead; for example, see a play instead of watching TV, play a board game instead of a video game, read a book instead of using social media.

Relational: Use entertainment to connect with someone. Let your kids teach you how to play their favorite video game. Watch your spouse's favorite show and learn about the characters. Ask your friends to share their favorite music with you.

GUIDED JOURNALING

Using the questions offered throughout the entry, journal about the negative and positive ways your entertainment choices impact your heart, soul, mind, body, and relationships.

WEEK 33
UNIFIED RELATIONSHIPS

Our unity is a reflected unity, an image of the Trinity's perfect
and eternal unity. And our unity is a redeemed unity, a unity
granted to us through Jesus's atoning work on the cross, by which
he brought sinners like you and me into his family.

Jonathan Holmes

We live in a divided world. Some days it feels impossible to find
common ground. A quick scroll through Facebook or Twitter
reveals a handful of topics on which Christians bitterly disagree.
Conversations about politics quickly descend into malicious
and vilifying words. Judgmental arguments about topics such
as government policies, health care, and matters of social justice
abound. Our commitment to our own views can create unnecessary divides and shut out those who disagree with our way of
thinking. Even topics of theology can lead to disunity. Who do
we baptize? What versions of the Bible should we use? What is
the role of men and women in the church? Unified relationships—even with other believers—can feel impossible to attain.

In the face of these challenges, Scripture unapologetically
calls us to persevere toward unity in Christ. Psalm 133:1 says,
"Behold, how good and pleasant it is when brothers dwell in
unity!" The word "behold" at the beginning of the verse is ba-
sically telling us to stop for a moment and look at our relationships. Psalm 133 tells us that unity is the active ingredient that

makes our relationships good and pleasant. We experience unity when we center our relationships on a shared faith and mutual goal of pleasing Christ and making him known.

Psalm 133 goes further to show us that the unity we experience in our relationships is a picture of the unity we experience with God. In Psalm 133:2 we are given a picture of Aaron, the priest, being covered with oil. This priestly act foreshadows the atoning work of Jesus. Just as the priest would be covered in oil and go before God on behalf of the people bringing unity again between God and man, Jesus brings that for believers. He allows us to be fully accepted by and united to God.

Pursuing unity does not mean that you will not have challenging conversations, differences of opinions, or need to stand up for your convictions. At times, we may need to distance ourselves from relationships that are harmful or abusive. We won't get into the best ways to approach challenging disagreements and relationships in this book. For our current purposes, consider how Christian unity relates to our topic of self-care. Unity is connected to our ability to care for each other in ways that benefit ourselves and our larger communities.

Unified relationships are characterized by encouraging and fulfilling interactions that leave us with more to offer others. With Christ as our center, all sorts of people with all sorts of opinions and beliefs come together. Despite our differences, we help each other through suffering, build up each other's faith, and work together for the glory of God and the good of his people. When we remember that the bonds of Christ are more important than our differing opinions, we create a context to relax, play, worship, and enjoy life in each other's company. Despite our differences, we can still experience good and pleasant relationships filled with happiness, humor, and enjoyment of one another.

GOSPEL SPOTLIGHT

John 13:35 says that people will know we belong to Jesus as they observe our love for each other. Our unity with other believers illustrates to the world our union with God, which is available to all through Jesus (John 17:21). Unity is not just for our good but also for the eternal good of others.

ACTION AND APPLICATION

Spiritual: Read Psalm 133. Think about your good, pleasant, and unified relationships with other believers. How do they remind you of the unity you have with God through Jesus?

Emotional: When you think about your relationships, do they bring good and pleasant feelings? Or, are you more likely to feel bitterness, anger, annoyance, disdain, or other more complicated emotions? Think of a good relationship. Write out a list of words that describe your feelings about it. Now think of a challenging relationship. What words describe your feelings about that relationship?

Physical: Create unity in your relationships through a physical gesture. Bring a coworker a cup of coffee. Buy lunch for a friend. Write an apology note. Make a meal or mow a lawn for someone who is struggling.

Relational: Identify one of your relationships that is marked by unity. Do something fun with that person this week. Who will you spend time with? What will you do together?

GUIDED JOURNALING

Think of a relationship that is not good and pleasant. Journal about what you could do to create more unity in this relationship.

WEEK 34
THE THORNS OF COMPARISON

What God has for you, no mortal being can take from you, so
you neither have to compete or compare.

Crawford Loritts

Comparison begins with the enjoyment of common ground.
You have a friend or colleague who has the same experience or
interests as you, or maybe you work together or serve in a similar
ministry. Or perhaps the commonality is based on being in the
same stage of life: launching a career, raising a family, or looking
toward retirement. The common ground draws you toward each
other. It is a beautiful landscape where friendship can flourish
and blessing can multiply.

But sometimes that common ground can take a turn toward
the dangerous path of comparison. You begin to weigh your
story against another's, and when it doesn't balance, thorns of
jealousy and pride start to grow. You no longer rejoice when you
hear of your colleague's accomplishment or success. The news of
your friend's unexpected blessing or opportunity stings like net-
tles as you veer away from the pleasant landscape of commonality down toward the prickled path of comparison.

If you have ever felt this way, you are not alone. Comparison
can lead us all to believe our efforts are less valuable. This breeds
doubt. You start to wonder if you are any good at anything.
If you continue down that path you will likely become lost in

self-absorbed thinking. You wonder if you should be doing what your friend is doing. You might begin to question your direction in life and reconsider what you felt called to do. The feelings of inferiority can make you want to distance yourself from the person who seems far more successful than you. Before you know it, you are entangled. The landscape is now filled with brambles all around, and getting out unscathed seems impossible.

We have all experienced comparison at some point. When this happens, Scripture helps us to correct the course and find our way back to where we need to be. In 1 Corinthians we have clear instruction on how to think about the work the Lord has called us to do: "This is how one should regard us, as servants of Christ and stewards of the mysteries of God. *Moreover, it is required of stewards that they be found faithful*" (1 Corinthians 4:1–2, emphasis added).

We are told to be faithful. To stay the course the Lord has mapped out for our particular life and calling should be our focus. We are to wisely steward our gifts and abilities, not compare them with others. God will judge the measure of our work, and he will give the appropriate praise (2 Corinthians 1:5). When we are faithful, we give no room for self-focused comparisons that leave us feeling insecure. Faithfulness is what's required. This will mean that some people will accomplish more than others. That is OK—we are to be steadfast. Some people's lives will seem to be filled with more blessings and benefits. That is OK—we are to be consistent and content. The humility of this mindset will allow us to rejoice when others are blessed as we focus not on ourselves or our perceived deficiencies but on being faithful to the One who has called us.

GOSPEL SPOTLIGHT

The Bible teaches us that our identity is to be found in Christ alone. Jesus has secured our standing before God and gives us all

we need. Allow that truth to reorient you when you are tempted
to wander toward the path of comparison.

ACTION AND APPLICATION

Spiritual: Read 1 Corinthians 4:1–7. Prayerfully consider
how comparison has affected your spiritual life.

Emotional: How has comparison impacted your emotional
well-being? Write down a list of feelings you experience when
you compare yourself with others.

Physical: Do you have any physical limitations that make
you feel less adequate to do the work God has given to you?
What does faithfulness look like within your physical limitations?

Relational: How does your engagement with people on social media tempt you toward comparison. Who in your life do
you compare yourself with? Notice how the comparison affects
your relationship with that person.

GUIDED JOURNALING

Write out a prayer to God to help you turn from the thorny
path of comparison toward the road of faithfulness. Based on
this prayer, what is one action you can take this week to focus
on being faithful?

WEEK 35
DEGREES OF FRIENDSHIP

Friendship halves our troubles and doubles our joys.

J. C. Ryle

Friendships are not created equal. Some friendships take more work than others. Some are forged through common interest; others are formed due to a shared task or responsibility; and some friendships are made unexpectedly in a more organic or providential way. You might have friends who feel closer than your own family. Other friends you may only talk to once a year at best, but despite the infrequent communication, you remain friends.

One common misunderstanding in Christian circles is that friendships, specifically with other believers, should all be marked by significant depth and closeness. It is not wrong to be closer with some people than you are with others. While all friendships don't need to have the same degree of depth, they all take intentionality and a willingness to be known.

Jesus himself showed us this. He was a "friend of sinners" and known by a wide variety of people with whom he shared meals and conversation. He also had closer friends like Lazarus, Mary, and Martha. In addition, he had the twelve disciples with whom he chose to engage in more intentional friendship and ministry. Out of the twelve, he had three—Peter, James, and John—he was even closer to. With those three, he went deeper, sharing unique moments and conversations not experienced with the other disciples. Of those three he had one who was closer still: John. John is described in Scripture as "the disciple whom Jesus loved." He was the one who laid on Jesus's breast at the last supper (John 13:23). All of these friendships were tied to the human need of companionship. We were made to be in community.

Jesus did not love John more than the other disciples even though he did share a closer friendship with him. This was not sinful exclusion; it was a naturally formed closeness. Not forced. Not obliged. But shared by only them.

Do believers have to be close friends with someone just because they are in the same Christian circles? Does the fact that we are all followers of Christ mean we must all be best friends? These questions can cause Christians undo stress and frustration. Instead we should consider how to make more natural connections with one another. In some cases, we may need to be more willing to be known; in other situations we can rest in the fact that a casual but genuine friendship is sufficient. Let the friendships of Jesus teach us that this variation is a natural part of life.

Don't exhaust yourself trying to be the closest of friends with all believers. Instead, be willing to engage, be vulnerable, and embrace the blessing and joy of varying levels of friendships.

GOSPEL SPOTLIGHT

As a Christian you are a friend of God. Jesus calls you friend. And this friendship is intimate and everlasting.

ACTION AND APPLICATION

Spiritual: Using Jesus's own life as an example, prayerfully evaluate the friendships God has given you. Spend time praying for and thanking God for the varying degrees of friendships that are gifts of companionship to your soul.

Emotional: Do you tend to share your deepest feelings with all your friends? Or do you tend to be overly guarded with your emotions? Healthy vulnerability will mean you make careful choices on how much to share and with whom. Wisely consider which of your friends should know more or less about your feelings. Friends who have proven trustworthy with small areas of vulnerability will likely be faithful with more.

Physical: Physical presence strengthens friendships. You catch more nonverbal communication when you are with someone. Plan some face-to-face time with a friend this week. Notice how being together in person strengthens your relationship.

Relational: Do you have a "John" in your life? Take some time this week to reach out to that friend and thank this person for the close friendship.

GUIDED JOURNALING

Consider how your own friendships vary in depth of closeness. List out the names of your friends. Include relationships that are casual acquaintances, closer companions, as well as those who are your dearest friends. As you reflect on this list, what does it reveal about your friendships? Journal your thoughts.

SECTION 5
WORK LIFE

WEEK 36
DANGERS OF SELF-DRIVEN WORKERS

Whatever you honor most will rule you. Honor what is best that
you may be governed by what is best.

The Sentences of Sextus

I (Eliza) grew up with a strong work ethic modeled by my amazing mother. She was a single mom with four children. She had
to work hard, and she taught us all to do the same. Working
was not something I dreaded; it was a satisfying means to an
end. From my early days of babysitting or mowing lawns, I was
taught to go beyond what was expected. Sure, I liked the cash in
my pocket, but I was motivated by a job well done.

I remember hearing a passage of Scripture in my late teens
that resonated with me and encouraged me in this pursuit of
hard work. "Whatever your hand finds to do, do it with your
might" (Ecclesiastes 9:10). I felt a sense of personal connection
with those words. I valued working hard, and when you value
something you pursue it. However, I didn't fully understand that
this passage is not intended to elevate work to be the driving
force in life. Work, like everything, needs to have its proper place
and boundaries.

God calls you to faithfully and diligently do your work.
Many passages speak to this (Proverbs 12:11; 13:4; Colossians
3:23–24). Yet, work should not be the ultimate focus and motivation in life. That is meant only for God. Anything that takes

that place violates the command to have no other gods besides the Lord (Exodus 20:3).

If you are self-driven, someone who needs little external motivation to take on a task, be cautious of a couple things. It can be easy to elevate work to an unhealthy place. For the self-driven person, work can become an identity or a god. It can become a means of validating your existence, rather than a means to worship and glorify God. The harder you work or the more you accomplish, the more validated you feel. This thinking is contrary to the gospel, which says your worth rests solely on the work Christ has done for you (Ephesians 2:8–9).

Another danger is when work is no longer a way to bless others but instead is a means of maintaining your false identity. There are subtle elements of selfishness behind every workaholic. Working may appear to be for the good of those you financially support when in actuality, it has more to do with you and how it makes you feel. God gives you your abilities and gifts so you can enrich others. This is the emphasis of 2 Corinthians 9:11. Your ability to work hard should always be used for the generous good of others.

While working hard can be an honorable quality, it's dangerous to make it what you honor or value most. That place belongs to God alone. Work, like everything, has its place and purpose. Our work is to bring glory to God. When the Lord is who you value most, your work becomes a way to honor him. Having this focus allows you to keep work in its proper place, which will lead to your own flourishing.

GOSPEL SPOTLIGHT

Read and meditate on Ephesians 2:8–9. "For by grace you have been saved through faith. And this is not your own doing; it is the gift of God, not a result of works, so that no one may boast."

ACTION AND APPLICATION

Spiritual: Are the first thoughts of your day about God or your work? Write a morning routine that starts your day with a focus on God.

Emotional: Do you feel most emotionally fulfilled when you are working or when you are communing with God? Reflect on what this may reveal about the place work holds in your life.

Physical: Do you push the limits of your physical health to do more work? What one way will you care for your physical needs this week in light of your work demands?

Relational: Pay attention to your work routine today. Does it hinder any of your relationships? Identify one change you can make to your work routine to prioritize the good of others.

GUIDED JOURNALING

How were you convicted by this week's entry? Write a prayer asking for God's help in the space below. For the rest of this week, start every day by praying this prayer.

WEEK 37
STEWARDING A STRONG AMBITION

Christians are to be fully engaged at work as whole persons,
giving their minds, hearts, and bodies fully to doing the best job
possible on the task at hand.

Timothy J. Keller

Many of our friends are go-getters. They run businesses and
work high-level corporate jobs. They are studying to be archi-
tects, doctors, and ministry leaders, or they already hold ad-
vanced degrees. Many of them do all of this on top of excelling
at the work of parenting and creating a home. We love watching
our friends accomplish great things.

In observing our friends, we have noticed Christians can
sometimes feel an undercurrent of shame when they have a
strong desire to excel in their fields and achieve lofty goals. People who have a healthy ambition to do radical things for the
Lord are sometimes admonished to slow down and be more like
Mary and less like Martha, creating additional guilt.

This caution is often necessary. Throughout this book, we offer
many encouragements to slow down, recognize your limitations,
and protect yourself from burnout. Each of these encouragements
remains important, but they also are not the whole story. When
approached in the right way, a strong drive to get things done can
be a wonderful gift. From the very beginning, God created people
to work (Genesis 1:28), and throughout Scripture, we see that

productivity in service to God and others is a worthy goal (Romans 12:11; Galatians 6:10; Titus 3:14). Maximizing our ability to do work that uplifts others and advances God's kingdom is one way we steward the gifts God has given us (1 Peter 4:10).

To thrive in your work and steward a strong ambition, start with assessing your motives. As you set goals, juggle a busy schedule, and seek to accomplish big things, be sure it's God you are serving. He is the one we work for. He is our master, and we should keep two responsibilities in mind as we use the gifts he has given us.

Our first responsibility is to work unto the Lord, not men (Colossians 3:23). If our motivation for working is to experience people's approval, we will run into problems. We will never be able to please everyone. Our schedules will lack limits and boundaries, and we will take on work that isn't meant for us. Work unto the Lord is more intentional and thoughtful because it is more prayerful. When our heart's focus is to serve the Lord in our work, he helps us thrive in the midst of busy schedules.

Our second responsibility is to serve others, not our own desires. Too often, we fill our schedules in ways that seem righteous on the surface but actually come from selfish motives. We take a job that makes us feel important, even though we know it will negatively impact our family. We say yes to requests so people won't feel bad and we won't feel uncomfortable, even though we know it will push our schedules past our limits. This approach to work is self-focused. It's not good for our hearts or the people we serve.

Stewarding a strong ambition well means putting God first and replacing selfish desires with a goal of truly doing what is best for others. With this in place, follow your ambitions freely.

GOSPEL SPOTLIGHT

Our hard work sometimes flows out of pride, selfish ambitions, and people pleasing tendencies. When our lives are rooted in the gospel, our ambitions to do much for the Lord flow out of our love for Jesus and our gratitude for what he has done for us.

ACTION AND APPLICATION

Spiritual: Each time you make decisions about adding work to your schedule, examine your heart. What is your motivation in saying no? What is your motivation in saying yes? Does your decision reflect a desire to serve God or please man?

Emotional: Journal about the emotions that tend to drive decisions about your work schedule. Are you prone to be motivated by fear? Guilt or shame? Pride? Or are you more often motivated by love for God and others?

Physical: Our brains need time and physical space to make good decisions about our schedules. The next time an opportunity comes up, you don't need to decide right away. Ask for a few hours or days to assess your motivation and think about your response.

Relational: When you make decisions about your work schedule, examine your heart as it relates to your relationships with people in your life. Are you seeking to serve your own desires or to serve the needs of others?

GUIDED JOURNALING

Consider your current schedule. Based on what you've learned this week, what do you feel compelled to change about your schedule?

WEEK 38
HIGH-FUNCTIONING BURNOUT

> Most people crack up because they try to do what God never
> intended them to do.
>
> *William Still*

In Week 11 you took a brief burnout assessment. Perhaps that week provided confirmation that pushing through has led you to burnout. But what if you took that assessment and didn't feel you were in danger? Maybe you regularly push through busy times of constant demands and just keep on going. Sometimes signs of burnout are hidden, even from ourselves. This week we are focusing on what we are going to call "high-functioning burnout."

High-functioning burnout is different from typical burnout in that the symptoms are not obvious and often a person doesn't get to a place of exhaustion leading to total shutdown. Instead, high-functioning burnout keeps a person serving and working until life is best described as a hamster wheel. People with high-functioning burnout may look like they have a lot of energy, but in reality they are just trying to catch their breath. They continue to willingly engage and are not apathetic. They are effective in their work but live with a level of stress that fuels their forward momentum. This experience is especially common among people in helping or ministry roles.

One reason Christians are prone to this is related to our natural tendency toward performance-based acceptance. Despite what Scripture teaches on grace, and contrary to the numerous books, sermons, or conferences on the topic, our natural disposition is to love the law and find acceptance in how well we keep it. We need to preach the gospel to ourselves daily and remind ourselves that we don't have to work for acceptance. A daily dose of what Jesus accomplished is needed in every believer's heart.

Another reason Christians are prone to high-functioning burnout is because followers of Jesus are called to exemplify sacrificial living. We are to lose our lives for Christ (Matthew 10:39). But we must keep in mind we are also called to be faithful to the end (Matthew 24:13). There are healthy and unhealthy ways to live selflessly. Choosing to meet ministry needs and serving others even when your schedule is filled to the brim is not always a healthy application of this call. While there are appropriate times to say yes to serving or ministering opportunities, saying yes to more than you should is not fruit of a self-sacrificing life. It may be evidence of a need for growth in wisdom and discernment. It may also point to the need to assess your motives in serving.

It is important to see how a wrong view of sacrificial living can create a continual push to do more and more. This push may not come all at once. It is often an accumulation of many compounded circumstances and requests. The longer you operate in this mode the more at risk you are for the burnout described in Week 11.

Jesus said he came that we may have life and that we would have it abundantly (John 10:10). This applies both to our eternal life with him in heaven but also to the time we have here on earth. Engaging in kingdom work does not come at the expense of a life of joy and peace. God's response to exhaustion is rest, not more work.

When symptoms of burnout show up and you keep pushing through, you can find yourself adjusting to the pace. Does the hamster wheel metaphor accurately fit your life? You can't get off, but you can't stop running either. Do the responsibilities of life feel like they are getting heavier but the only solution is to carry it alone? Do you willingly add more to your already busy schedule? If this describes you, you may be living with high-functioning burnout.

GOSPEL SPOTLIGHT

Matthew 11:28–30 reminds us that we find rest for our souls in Jesus. Our rest is not found in all the work we can get done but in the work of Jesus on our behalf. Take a moment to read this passage. Is your soul resting in Jesus?

ACTION AND APPLICATION

Spiritual: Saying yes to another serving opportunity does not make God more pleased with you. Meditate on Philippians 3:9 and ask the Lord to help you rest in the righteousness that is yours in Christ.

Emotional: High-functioning burnout can lead you to detach from your emotions. Take some time to notice if you have dismissed or ignored your emotions in your efforts to juggle your responsibilities.

Physical: In Week 14 you were encouraged to make needed appointments for your physical health. People experiencing high-functioning burnout will naturally push these appointments to the lowest place on their list. This week make whatever appointments you may be neglecting.

Relational: Do people commonly make comments to you such as, "I don't know how you do all you do" or "I get exhausted just watching you"? If so, consider that others may be seeing your "hamster wheel" reality. Ask them if they have any concerns about your pace. Listen carefully to their input.

GUIDED JOURNALING

People prone to high-functioning burnout look successful on the outside but feel internally overwhelmed. Reconciling this dissonance requires a willingness to be both honest and vulnerable. Think about someone you could share your internal struggles with. Use this week's journaling to write what you could share with a trusted friend in order to move toward vulnerability about how your pace in life actually affects you.

WEEK 39
THE REWARDS OF HARD WORK

Our work ought to show we have a higher calling. It ought to
say that something greater than earthly reward motivates it.

Keith Welton

As a young teenager, I (Esther) was excited to start my first job.
For several months, I lived in Iowa and detasseled corn. Working
alongside dozens of other teens, our goal as a group was to sys-
tematically walk through cornfields and pull the tassels off each
cornstalk. Detasseling corn in this way promotes cross-pollina-
tion between fields. As the summer wore on, each day felt more
exhausting than the previous one. We would start before dawn
and work no matter the conditions. Trudging through mud.
Shivering through rain. Burning in the sun. The work was gruel-
ing, but I loved it. How can something so miserable feel so good?

Sometimes it just feels good to work hard. Busy seasons often
leave us longing for a moment to catch our breath, but as soon
as life slows down, it's easy to miss the work that previously felt
overwhelming. The end of a long vacation leaves us ready to get
back to the office. An extended sickness reveals that hard work is
a blessing not to be taken for granted. Those who experience the
loss of a job know that an empty schedule, with no routine or
tasks to keep you productive, can often lead to discouragement.

Work is good for us. It keeps our minds and bodies active.
It can get us out of the house and provide a setting for social

interaction. Self-care is not all about rest and relaxation. Too much downtime can leave us feeling bored, agitated, and depressed. We need balance in our lives, and working hard, especially in service to God and others, can be life-giving.

Refreshing others refreshes us (Proverbs 11:25). We find this truth repeated throughout Scripture. Jesus told his disciples, "Give, and it will be given to you. . . . For with the measure you use it will be measured back to you" (Luke 6:38). These Scriptures are not describing an automatic return of investment. This is not karma or the prosperity gospel. Rather, these verses describe a common pattern. In money, in relationships, in life, and in service, we reap what we sow (2 Corinthians 9:6). When we are faithful to use our gifts, God often entrusts us with more resources so we can continue stewarding them for the growth of his kingdom (see Matthew 25:14–30).

Working hard can be a way to care for ourselves. It often leads to great reward. Finishing a hard day's labor can be invigorating. To look back and know that we worked hard for the Lord and for other people can bring a sense of satisfaction. It's rewarding to see other people flourish as a result of our service. What's more, when our hard work blesses others, people are often drawn to bless us in return (2 Corinthians 9:12–14).

While earthly reward should not be our sole motivation for working hard, God often blesses us in surprising ways when our eyes are fixed on faithful service. When we give generously, God often gives generously back. Many times, God blesses our efforts of service in ways that not only refresh us, but also allow us to give more than we were able to before.

GOSPEL SPOTLIGHT

Jesus is the ultimate example of how sacrificial work leads to great reward. Jesus endured the pain of the cross not only because it was the will of the Father, but also "for the joy set before him"

(Hebrews 12:2 NIV). He looked beyond the pain of the cross to the end when he would accomplish his purposes for us, be reunited with his Father, and experience glorification in heaven.

ACTION AND APPLICATION

Spiritual: God does not guarantee that he will bless us with the health, money, or relationships we want in this lifetime. He does promise to reward us in heaven according to the deeds we have done (Revelation 22:12). How can this encourage you if your work doesn't seem to be reaping benefits right now?

Emotional: How would you describe your feelings toward the daily work God has called you to? How might these feelings either hinder or assist your ability to experience reward in your work?

Physical: Hard physical labor or mundane physical tasks such as mowing the lawn or washing the dishes can provide reward or rejuvenation. These tasks allow us to feel the satisfaction of bringing order to our lives and lead us to observe how much service of this kind blesses others. The next time you engage in this type of work remember how even tedious tasks can be a means of serving God and others.

Relational: List a couple people in your life you regularly serve. What blessings have you received in return as a result of your service to them?

GUIDED JOURNALING

Think about a time when you experienced the rewards of hard work. Journal about your experience in detail. How did God use work to reward, rejuvenate, or refresh you?

WEEK 40
DIVVY THE DUTY

Alone we can do so little, together we can do so much.

Helen Keller

My (Eliza) journey into ministry started in a small counseling center. Considering all we provided for churches and individuals, one would think we were a much larger operation. Despite being small, our reach was significant.

We had a small budget and since we were unable to hire support staff, I wore many hats. On paper I was the executive director. Practically, I was the director of counseling, the director of operations, the director of finance, the office administrator, and a counselor all at the same time. Thanks to the input of others, this season of juggling multiple responsibilities taught me a necessary lesson.

One morning, a friend of the ministry stopped in to say hello. I was busy filling candy dishes in our counseling rooms when she popped in. Seeing what I was doing, she asked me a simple question, "Why are you doing that?" I knew she was not looking for the obvious answer. Instead she was asking why *I* was doing that when someone else could. The problem was, I did not have anyone else to ask. All my counselors were carrying a full load. Who else would do it?

My vision was too small, and she helped broaden it. Her comment turned into a conversation, which became a plan to utilize volunteers in the ministry. As I learned to divvy up these duties to others, I noticed a surprising benefit. It did not just bless me; it blessed others as well. The counselors had increased access to me and could get more support. I was able to use my ministry gifts to focus on counseling and teaching so more people were helped. The volunteers found a place of connection and purpose as they served each week.

A short time after bringing on volunteers, a passage in my Bible reading reminded me that the early church faced this same dilemma.

> Now in these days when the disciples were increasing in number, a complaint by the Hellenists arose against the Hebrews because their widows were being neglected in the daily distribution. And the twelve summoned the full number of the disciples and said, "It is not right that we should give up preaching the word of God to serve tables. Therefore, brothers, pick out from among you seven men of good repute, full of the Spirit and of wisdom, whom we will appoint to this duty." (Acts 6:1–3)

I was hired as the director of the ministry because of my counseling and leadership gifts. I didn't mind filling candy dishes, answering phones, or scheduling, but delegating these responsibilities freed me to focus on the work I was called to do. The lesson of sharing the workload gave me more bandwidth to fulfill my calling and responsibilities.

I trust I'm not the only one who has gotten lost in the thousand little jobs that take our focus from the main work we are called to do. Maybe you are a pastor who spends hours on administrative work that could be done by a willing volunteer. Or maybe, you are in a small ministry like I described and the operational tasks are absorbing all your time. Maybe you're a busy mom who is juggling being the teacher, cook, housecleaner, chief financial officer, and nurse to your family. Perhaps some of those duties could be shared with others in the house, a mother's helper, or even by someone hired to help a few hours here and there. Whatever your circumstance, take some time to consider how you may be able to divvy the duty.

GOSPEL SPOTLIGHT

Responsibilities can overwhelm us and distract us from the fact that God wants us to be at peace. The only way we can be at peace is to rest fully in the reality that our whole life is kept in Jesus (1 Thessalonians 5:23–24). He does not get overwhelmed and is never overworked, and he will finish the work he started.

ACTION AND APPLICATION

Spiritual: Prayerfully ask the Lord to show you where you may need to bring others into your life to help you.

Emotional: Write down what emotions come up when you think about sharing some of your responsibilities with others. What do these emotions reveal?

Physical: Often our bodies tell us when we are carrying more than we should. Notice any stress, strain, or symptom that may be connected to your attempt to do too much on your own.

Relational: Read 1 Corinthians 3:8–10. Make a list of people who could come alongside you in your work. Make a point to reach out to at least one person this week.

GUIDED JOURNALING

Using the bullet journal method, make a list of duties you are doing now that you feel you could share with someone else. Use this list when you reach out to someone this week.

WEEK 41
YOU ARE NOT YOUR JOB TITLE

No work, no matter how significant, is sufficient grounds to
gain access to God, nor can any work be the foundation of your
identity. The source and foundation of identity are in God, God's
grace, and God's having created humans in his own image.

Klyne R. Snodgrass

"What do you do?" It's a common question when people first
meet. To get to know someone, we want to know how they
spend their time. A job title feels like a concise way to sum up
who a person is and what that person might be like.

I (Esther) am often curious about what people do for a living. At the same time, I wish this personal question were not a
standard conversation starter. For many, it's a loaded question.
Personally, there have been times in my life when I was not able
to work. People would ask me this question, and I would feel
uncomfortable. What should I say? It felt as if my whole identity
was about to be summed up in the fact that I did not have a job.
If I wasn't working, who was I, and what did I do?

Jumping forward to the present, when people ask me what
I do now, I feel good about my answer. I like being a counselor
and a writer, and I feel proud of my work. While this is not bad
in and of itself, it is a slippery slope. At times, it's too easy for me
to place my identity in my accomplishments and feel like my job
titles are the most accurate descriptors of who I am.

When a job becomes our core identity, how we feel about ourselves begins to correspond with our perceived levels of success. In seasons when we don't have a job or on days when work goes poorly, we can feel depressed and anxious. We may quickly identify as a failure. Other days, when work goes well, our success can serve as the source of our happiness and peace. Our accomplishments become the litmus test for our meaning.

It's dangerous to make work the basis of our identity or the root of our satisfaction. God does not promise that we will be successful at our jobs or that we will be able to continue doing work that feels meaningful. More importantly, finding our identity in a job title can become idolatrous, and God calls us to give our whole allegiance to him. Whether you are a doctor, pastor, business owner, mother, grocery store manager, student, or unemployed worker, this is not the core of who you are. The core of your being—your identity that no job can add to or take away from—is the fact that you are God's child (John 1:12) and a fellow heir of Christ (Romans 8:17). You have been justified and redeemed (Romans 3:24) and through Christ have become the righteousness of God (2 Corinthians 5:21).

Believing these truths from Scripture can help us care for ourselves better. When our identity is grounded in Christ, we don't need the success of work to feel worthy. We stop feeling anxious and depressed when work does not go the way we want. Instead of striving for unnecessary accomplishments, we desire a more balanced life that attends to the health of our bodies, souls, minds, and relationships. As often happens when we align our lives with Scripture, we find that what God wants for us is also what is most healthy for us.

GOSPEL SPOTLIGHT

Our identity is grounded in what Christ has done for us. His justifying work makes us who we are. We are "in Christ." Our identity flows out of who he is and what he has accomplished on our behalf.

ACTION AND APPLICATION

Spiritual: In your own words, describe what it means to place your identity in Christ.

Emotional: Take note of any mood fluctuations that occur in relation to how well you perform at work. What are these mood fluctuations telling you?

Physical: Placing your identity in your work can lead to workaholism, which negatively impacts your body. In what ways, if any, has placing your identity in your work impacted your body?

Relational: Think about other questions you can ask when you meet someone new. What questions might help move conversations away from the common pitfall of identifying people based on their job titles?

GUIDED JOURNALING

How would you introduce yourself if you were to leave out your job titles, academic accomplishments, and daily work? Write out a description, and then take note of how you feel toward yourself, minus your work. What signs, if any, reveal that you are overidentifying with your job title or work accomplishments?

WEEK 42
"I CAN'T, BUT I CAN"

Creatures, by definition, are less than their Creator. He is
infinite, we are finite; he is unlimited, we are limited.

David P. Murray

One of the most important self-care strategies I (Esther) use on
a regular basis is setting healthy boundaries. While the word
boundary is not found in Scripture, we find this term helpful to
describe how we respond to Scripture's encouragement to recognize our limitations (see Week 11 and Week 22). Because I
deal with physical symptoms that become exacerbated if I do
too much, I have to be careful about what I agree to do. Even if
you don't deal with similar health problems, setting boundaries
is important to your long-term health and well-being.

Sometimes people struggle with that idea. Setting clear
boundaries might make you wonder if you aren't being loving
and sacrificial enough, but that does not need to be the case.
There are healthy and loving ways to set boundaries, and I want
to give you one specific strategy that has helped me in this area.

When people ask me to do something that I cannot or
should not do, I often say, "I can't do _____, but I can do
_____." This keeps me open to opportunities to serve but still
acknowledges I can't and shouldn't be doing everything. Sometimes I will give a reason for why I can't fulfill the initial request,

and other times I won't. Here are a few examples of what that can look like.

I can't meet with you at 8 p.m., but I can meet with you any day before 5 p.m. next week.

I can't serve on the hospitality committee, because I'm not available every week, but I can serve monthly on the prayer team.

I can't read you five more stories at bedtime, but I can read you one.

I can't work late tonight, because my son has a baseball game, but I can come in early tomorrow morning.

This strategy for setting boundaries is helpful for a few reasons. First, it recognizes our limitations and helps us practice humility. There are some things we cannot do. Saying, "I can't" is a practical way to not think more highly of ourselves then we should (Romans 12:3). We enter dangerous territory when we believe we are the only one able to get the work done. What we have to offer is but one small contribution to the limitless resources God has to draw on.

Second, this strategy recognizes that sometimes people have expectations of us that don't match God's expectations for us. It's easy to say yes simply because we don't want to upset anyone. Other times we start valuing the praise of people over the praise of God (John 12:43). When people's approval becomes more important than God's glory, we lose sight of the specific work God has for us.

Boundaries are not meant to be rigid fences that no one can ever breach. We aren't setting boundaries because we are trying to avoid work or don't want to inconvenience ourselves. Boundaries help us steward the specific resources God has given us. They enable us to contribute without overextending ourselves and redirect our energy to areas that best suit our gifts and abilities. Often this ends up being better for the people we serve, as it enables us to give the best of ourselves instead of spreading ourselves too thin.

GOSPEL SPOTLIGHT

We depend on a God who never has to say, "I can't." His immeasurable power that raised Jesus from the dead lives inside of us (Ephesians 1:19–20). Our limitations lead us to rely on God, who is faithful to provide what we need.

ACTION AND APPLICATION

Spiritual: Take a look at your schedule. Practice humility and depend on God's limitless resources by setting one new boundary this week.

Emotional: Sometimes we say yes when we should say no because we don't want to experience uncomfortable feelings. What uncomfortable feelings are you most prone to try and avoid?

Physical: Set a physical boundary in your calendar this week. For example, not working past _____ or not working more than ___ hours a week.

Relational: Practice using this statement with someone this week: "I can't _____. But, I can _____."

GUIDED JOURNALING

Journal through some ways you can use boundaries to steward your resources so you can more wisely distribute them to others and redirect your energy to those tasks that best suit your gifts and abilities.

WEEK 43
THE BLESSINGS OF
HEALTHY RHYTHMS

We are designed for a rhythm of work and rest.

Andy Crouch

A rhythm is simply a nuanced way of describing the routines and habits in our lives. They can be as mundane as a morning cup of coffee or as mindless as scrolling through our phone at the start of the day. Our work is one area of life where rhythms naturally evolve. These rhythms are significant because they reveal our priorities. They drive our hearts and determine our actions. Establishing healthy rhythms in work can be challenging.

Like us, you have rhythms to your workday. For me (Eliza) I start most of my days with a morning prayer walk. This healthy rhythm orients my heart before diving into the demands of the day. However, an unhealthy routine I unwittingly practice is to eat lunch in front of my computer. This causes me to ignore the need for healthy breaks in my workday.

For me (Esther) one unhealthy rhythm I can fall into is checking my email first thing in the morning. This habit draws me into the stress of work first thing. A much healthier rhythm that I strive for is to eat breakfast and spend time with the Lord before starting my responsibilities. Intentionally choosing to care for my body and soul first sets me up for a much better day.

This week we are going to see how two healthy rhythms can be a blessing when they become a regular part of our work week.

Rhythm One: Notice what is good. We don't have to read far into Scripture to see this rhythm modeled for us in relation to work. Genesis chapter 1 has a felt rhythm to it. Take a moment to read the chapter right now. At the end of each day we see a recognition of the work done and this repeated phrase: "And God saw that it was good" (Genesis 1:10). This little phrase reminds us to take time to regularly notice good moments in our workday.

In a season when both my husband and I (Eliza) worked from home, we intentionally paused throughout the day to share what was going well. This rhythm became a helpful reminder of how God blesses us with good things even in the midst of a hectic and demanding workday.

Rhythm Two: Pause to turn Godward. In much of the Old Testament we see regular rhythms that interrupt work. People in biblical times had good reason to work continually. If they did not work, they would likely die. They could not depend on well-stocked grocery stores or online shopping for essentials in life. Though costly, in the midst of the essential work, they carried out rhythms of pause.

In describing his experience of reading the Old Testament, Carey Nieuwhof says, "There is a forced rhythm of rest in the Old Testament that grinds you to a halt and into the presence of God regularly."[12] We see this in all the festivals, feasts, offerings, and observances. These routine pauses were embedded into a life filled with work. Our work also must include rhythms that orient our hearts to God.

Rhythms reprioritize our day. They allow us to attend to our work while keeping a Godward focus. These healthy rhythms help us give attention to the Lord in the midst of a busy life and provide rich blessings to our souls.

GOSPEL SPOTLIGHT

As you take time to notice what is good, call to mind the fact that in Jesus we have been given the greatest good in all of life. The reality of our salvation is the most amazing good and is well worth bringing into the spotlight of our day on a regular basis.

ACTION AND APPLICATION

Spiritual: This week create space in your workday to pause and connect with the Lord. At the start or end of your day, or during your lunch hour or break, take five to ten minutes to pray and commit your efforts to him. Do this every day this week and notice the impact it has on you spiritually. Check off each day to help you keep on track.

- ☐ Sunday
- ☐ Monday
- ☐ Tuesday
- ☐ Wednesday
- ☐ Thursday
- ☐ Friday
- ☐ Saturday

Emotional: Rhythms can help us make good decisions that are not driven by our emotions. What healthy rhythm do you need to practice in your work life when your emotions pull you elsewhere? (For example: Take a walk before a stress-inducing meeting. Pray and take some deep breaths before interacting with a stubborn child or difficult coworker.)

Physical: This week as you pause to spend time with God during your workday, physically posture yourself in prayer however you are able: kneel, close your eyes, lift your hands. Aligning your body with your heart and mind provides more attentive engagement.

Relational: Incorporating new rhythms can be easier when you do so with a friend. Choose someone to share your plans with this week. Ask them to pray for you as you incorporate these rhythms. Consider asking them to join you in implementing new rhythms.

GUIDED JOURNALING

Write out a plan for how you will apply the two healthy rhythms in your work this week: (1) Notice what is good, and (2) pause to turn toward God. At the end of the week go back and notice any blessings these rhythms brought to your life.

WEEK 44

SEASONS OF INTENSE WORK

If Jesus gives us a task or assigns us to a difficult season, every
ounce of our experience is meant for our instruction and
completion if only we'll let Him finish the work.

Beth Moore

As you read this book, it's possible you feel frustrated by all this
talk about self-care. It doesn't escape you that you are starting to
burn out. More than anything, you would like to work less and
spend more time taking care of yourself. However, as you honestly assess your life and responsibilities, you feel fairly certain
this is impossible.

I've experienced seasons like this myself. Completing the
requirements for my (Esther's) counseling licensure was filled
with demands and challenges. Nearing the end of the process,
exhausted and depleted, I faced a choice. I could keep going,
even though I was burning out. Or, I could stop to take care of
myself and miss the deadline for completion. The task was hard,
but the decision was not. It was clear God had put me on this
path, so for a season, I pushed through. Looking back, I know I
made the right choice.

It's likely you have faced similarly challenging times. Perhaps you are the only person who is able to care for your ailing
parents. Or, you are finishing up seminary while working a full-
time job, and no one can do the work for you. As the caretaker of

a new baby, there is no way to escape the fact that you are on call 24/7. As an executive, you find yourself rising early and staying up late to close out your fiscal year. Self-care can feel impossible during seasons such as these.

Ecclesiastes 3:1 says, "For everything there is a season, and a time for every matter under heaven." This includes seasons of intense work. Sometimes our bodies and minds struggle as a result of the work God asks us to do. Self-denial for the good of our families, ministries, and the spread of the gospel can be necessary (Luke 9:23). We see this modeled in the ministries of people throughout Scripture. Paul is a prime example—he faced hardship upon hardship for the sake of spreading the gospel (2 Corinthians 11:22–28). How should we approach caring for ourselves when pushing through seems necessary for the good of others?

One answer to this question lies in doing our best to ensure that these times remain seasons, not lifelong patterns. Seasons do not last forever. They end at some point. There is a time to sacrifice, and a time to rest; a time to push our bodies, and a time to stop. It is also important to be honest with ourselves. We need to search our hearts and make sure that these intense levels of work are actually necessary. We need to humble ourselves and ask for help. Perhaps most important is assessing our motives. Are we truly offering our bodies as sacrifices to God (Romans 12:1), or are we sacrificing ourselves for our own glory (Matthew 23:5)?

Life felt difficult as I worked toward counseling licensure, but looking back, I see innumerable ways God met me and gave me what I needed to finish. The license I received allows me to serve people in ways that would otherwise be impossible. I'm glad I pushed through, but as soon as that season finished, I made changes to my schedule to make space for a summer of rejuvenating rest. In difficult seasons, God helps us persevere. He also gives wisdom to know what changes we might need to make in order to move into a less frenzied pace.

GOSPEL SPOTLIGHT

Seasons of self-denial can take us to places beyond our ability to endure (2 Corinthians 1:8). Here, we are united to Christ and his suffering. Suffering for the good of others allows us to know Christ and the power of his resurrection (Philippians 3:10). Let this encourage you in difficult seasons.

ACTION AND APPLICATION

Spiritual: Assess the motives behind any sacrifices you are making. Are you truly sacrificing for the good of others? Or, are you sacrificing to make yourself look good or for other wrong motives?

Emotional: During seasons of necessary and intense work, emotional and mental needs sometimes go unmet. Share your emotional and mental needs with God right now and ask him to sustain you.

Physical: Even when you cannot prioritize your physical health, stay aware of what your body is doing. Take a moment to do a body scan as described in the appendix. What do you notice? Address any physical concerns as soon as you are able.

Relational: Ask your family how your work is impacting them. If you are facing an intense season of responsibility, ask them how long they feel able to sacrifice along with you. Reassure them that this season will not last forever.

GUIDED JOURNALING

If you are going through a season of intense work or responsibility, come up with a game plan. Sit down with your family, a friend, or a mentor and determine if this season is actually necessary. If it is not, what changes will you make starting today? If it is necessary, write out what you need to get through and your plan for when it might end.

SECTION 6
A RESTFUL LIFE

WEEK 45
REMEMBER THE SABBATH

[The Sabbath] is not an interlude, but the climax of living.

Rabbi Abraham Joshua Heschel

Growing up, my (Esther's) family kept the Sabbath in a literal sense. Sunday was for morning church, eating a meal together, resting, and evening church. It was not for catching up on school, organized sports, watching TV, or completing unnecessary work. Over the years, I entered new communities that did not share these same convictions about Sabbath-keeping, and this prompted me to study this practice for myself.

In my reading, I was most impacted by Jesus's words: "the Sabbath was made for man, not man for the Sabbath" (Mark 2:27). God created the Sabbath for us. No matter your views on whether or not we *have* to take this day, the point is that we *get* to take this day. For one day out of the week—whether that happens on Sunday or some other day—God invites you to cease your normal routine and focus more fully on two important parts of life.

First, the Sabbath is an opportunity to focus on worshiping God. While connecting with God should happen all week long, one day is set aside as holy and to be observed for the Lord. On this day of sacred assembly (Leviticus 23:3), we gather with other believers to encourage one another, pray together, and worship the Lord with one voice.

Second, the Sabbath is an opportunity to rest from work (see Exodus 20:8–11). The Sabbath is not a burden or one more legalistic item to add to a long to-do list. It is the gift of rest. From creation, God ordered each week to include one day without work. In addition to worship, the Sabbath is a day to sleep, play, socialize, and engage in other rejuvenating aspects of life that often get pushed aside.

Focused rest and worship on the Sabbath remind us of the promise of eternal rest. Read this passage from Hebrews. It may feel tempting to skim through, but we encourage you to slowly read the text.

> Therefore, while the promise of entering his rest still stands, let us fear lest any of you should seem to have failed to reach it. For good news came to us just as to them, but the message they heard did not benefit them, because they were not united by faith with those who listened. For we who have believed enter that rest, as he has said, "As I swore in my wrath, 'They shall not enter my rest,'" although his works were finished from the foundation of the world. For he has somewhere spoken of the seventh day in this way: "And God rested on the seventh day from all his works." And again in this passage he said, "They shall not enter my rest." Since therefore it remains for some to enter it, and those who formerly received the good news failed to enter because of disobedience, again he appoints a certain day, "Today," saying through David so long afterward, in the words already quoted, "Today, if you hear his voice, do not harden your hearts." For if Joshua had given them rest, God would not have spoken of another day later on. So then, there remains a Sabbath rest for the people of God, for whoever has entered God's rest has also rested from his works as God did from his. Let us therefore

strive to enter that rest, so that no one may fall by the
same sort of disobedience. (Hebrews 4:1–11)

Our bodies and souls function best when provided with adequate time for rest and worship. Resting our bodies is a physical
reminder that the work we do the other six days of the week does
not save us. Worshiping God acknowledges that true rest for our
souls is found only in him. Through keeping the Sabbath, we
embody our confession that it is Jesus—not the works of our
hands—who makes us right with God.

GOSPEL SPOTLIGHT

Jesus accomplished rest for our souls on the cross. Allow your
Sabbath rest this week to remind you of the eternal rest you will
one day experience.

ACTION AND APPLICATION

Spiritual: Read the following passages on the Sabbath: Exodus 20:8–11; Deuteronomy 5:12–14; Mark 2:23–28; Hebrews
4:1–11. Based on these passages, what do you think it means to
keep the Sabbath? Does your functional approach to keeping the
Sabbath each week align with what you find in Scripture?

Emotional: Next Sabbath, notice how intentional rest and
worship impact your emotions. How does rest affect you emotionally? How does worship affect you emotionally?

Physical: What physically rejuvenates you? Think of one
way you can interrupt your regular physical routine and engage
in needed rest or recreation.

Relational: The Sabbath is an opportunity to join with
other believers to worship God together. Remember that missing corporate worship services impacts your own spiritual walk
as well as the whole body.

GUIDED JOURNALING

If you didn't read the Hebrews passage, read it now. Are you resting in Jesus? In what ways do you need to rest from your own works?

WEEK 46
SAVORING SMALL JOYS
AND SIMPLE PLEASURES

Whenever God reveals His nature in a new way, it is always
for a purpose. When He encounters you, He is allowing you to
know Him by experience.

Henry T. Blackaby

A firepit sits in my (Esther) small backyard. Fashioned from
bricks, the bottom layered with red gravel, it is only a few
dozen steps from our back door. In the first half of 2020, when
COVID-19 turned the world upside down, I and my husband
often found ourselves returning to this fireside retreat. Life became limited when we were asked to stay home for the safety of
all. We were unable to visit friends, go to church, go out to eat,
or travel as we pleased. With these familiar options no longer
possible, we looked for comforting replacements. Sitting outside
and enjoying a fire became a favorite.

The comfort of a fire did not take away our problems. A
pandemic still raged. Many people we knew were still suffering.
Our normal life struggles persisted, complicated by new fears
of potential illness. Even so, for a few hours on many cool late
afternoons, we would sit and experience the fact that even a pandemic could not erase life's small gifts. God's goodness could
still be found in the taste of a s'more, the heat of smoldering red

coals, the sight of our dogs playing, the smell of hot dogs roasting, and the sound of our own laughter.

God designed us to know him and his goodness experientially. We see this in Psalm 34:8, which invites us to "taste and see that the LORD is good!" We experience the goodness of God through our senses. Our bodies allow us to more fully encounter the world he has created. Enjoying simple pleasures is an important means of self-care that keeps us healthy and balanced. Taking time for activities we enjoy can restore stamina to our bodies. Slowing down creates space to connect with God and can restore us spiritually. Savoring these moments often provides a mental break, restoring our minds for the work we eventually return to.

At different times in life, we may face barriers that prevent us from enjoying the types of leisure we desire. A new baby interrupts an active social life. Financial strains make certain hobbies impossible. Chronic health struggles limit activities we once enjoyed. Depression and anxiety steal our desire to participate in what once brought joy. Limitations such as these will rightly lead us to feel sad and disappointed, but these barriers to leisure are invitations to a greater awareness of the small joys and simple pleasures that surround us.

Joy is possible even when life is difficult and limited, because no matter our circumstances, the unfailing love of God fills the earth (Psalm 33:5). His goodness is all around us. We can more intentionally take note of his goodness by stopping and engaging our senses. What good things surround you now? The sound of your children playing? A cool breeze through the window? The savory aroma of soup simmering on the stove? Whatever your circumstances are today, taste and see the goodness of God. Hear, feel, and smell that his loving-kindness fills the earth. The more you pay attention, the more you will sense small gifts in your daily life that can become gateways to gratitude and joy.

GOSPEL SPOTLIGHT

As you pay attention to all of God's good gifts to you, remember his gift of grace, expressed in his kindness to us through Christ Jesus (Ephesians 2:7). In the age to come, we will experience the "incomparable riches of this grace" in ways we can only now imagine.

ACTION AND APPLICATION

Spiritual: Every good gift comes from God (James 1:17). The next time you enjoy a good gift, close your eyes, experience the pleasure of that moment, and say a thank-you to God for his blessings.

Emotional: Savor moments that elicit joy, happiness, peace, contentment, hope, love, or wonder. The next time you feel a pleasing emotion, pause for a moment and name what you are feeling. Close your eyes and savor the gift that led you to feel that way.

Physical: Use your five senses to experience the good gifts God has given you in this moment. Right now, what good and pleasing things can you see, hear, smell, taste, and touch?

Relational: How can you get creative with people in your life about finding God's good gifts even when life is limited? Try a new activity with someone you love this week.

GUIDED JOURNALING

Thank God for the small joys and simple pleasures in your life. Lord, I thank you for . . .

WEEK 47
ANXIOUS AND AWAKE

Stabilize your soul with the sovereignty of God. He reigns
supreme over every detail of the universe.

Max Lucado

Lying down in bed for the night, your mind begins to race. From
the moment you turn off the lights and set your phone aside,
you are pulled into an onslaught of thoughts. Everything that
happened today and all you need to do tomorrow now flashes
through your mind. Should I have handled that conversation
differently? Am I forgetting something? Will I have time to get
everything done?

Most people can recall nights like these. For some, they are a
regular occurrence. In my own (Esther) experience, these nights
sometimes happen when I am worried about a specific task or
problem. Other times I'm not anxious about anything in particular. On the surface, my thoughts seem neutral, but I still can't
sleep because my brain just won't stop running. Both kinds of
racing thoughts typically mean I am feeling overwhelmed. Even
when we are not consciously worried about an outcome, this
invasion of thoughts often signals that stress and anxiety lurk
beneath the surface.

Do you struggle to set your to-do list aside each evening?
Do thoughts of what you need to do tomorrow tend to keep you
awake? Try as you might, does it feel impossible to turn off your
brain? These can be important signs we should not ignore.

On those nights when we can't fall asleep, replaying all the work yet to be done, we need a reminder that God is in control and that he will accomplish his purposes in and through us. Sleep is an act of faith that recognizes God as the creator and sustainer of all the work we do during the day. Psalm 127:1 reminds us, "Unless the Lord builds the house, those who build it labor in vain." Because God is upholding the world, we can set our to-do list to the side and welcome restful sleep. God invites us to set aside an anxiety-driven life and to rest in the knowledge that "he gives sleep to the one he loves" (Psalm 127:2 CSB).

It's important to note that insomnia has many causes, and struggling to fall asleep does not equal a failure to trust in God. Sometimes insomnia is caused by physical factors such as prescription medication, hormonal changes, sleep apnea, chronic pain, and various other medical conditions. If your problem with insomnia persists, consider seeing a doctor to rule out or address causes such as these. Regardless of the cause of your insomnia, various strategies that impact your physical body can help. To aid your natural sleep-wake cycle, you might avoid using your phone and other screens at least thirty minutes before going to bed. Many people find that using a weighted blanket helps them feel calmer and fall asleep faster. Other strategies such as limiting caffeine, getting plenty of exercise during the day, and waking up at the same time each morning can also make a big difference.

Psalm 127 is not saying that all cases of insomnia signal a lack of faith or trust. It is, however, alerting us to *one* type of sleeplessness that can arise when we struggle to trust God with our unfinished work and unresolved problems. God invites us to remember that he is in control. He alone ensures that the work he wants to accomplish will get done. We can rest in this. Our to-do list can wait until tomorrow.

If you struggle to mentally turn off your brain at night, a few strategies can help. Try journaling everything you are thinking for ten minutes right before going to bed. You might mentally set aside your to-do list by taking each item and visualizing yourself giving it to God. Meditating on a favorite verse or reciting your favorite passage of Scripture can be helpful focusing activities. As we use strategies like this to let go, we create a better context for falling into a restorative sleep that will ready us to join God in the work he has waiting for us the next day.

GOSPEL SPOTLIGHT

When we are anxious and awake, we are prone to forget the promises of God secured for us through Jesus. The next time you experience difficulty falling asleep, use it as an opportunity to remember what Christ has done for you and thank him for your salvation.

ACTION AND APPLICATION

Spiritual: Are you rising up early and staying up late in vain? To what extent is your work driven by anxiety instead of grounded in trusting the Lord?

Emotional: Mentally set aside your to-do list each night. As you lie in bed, preparing for sleep, imagine your to-do list in your mind. Take each item and visualize yourself giving it to God for the night.

Physical: You just read about various strategies that can help prepare your body for sleep. Try just one of them this week.

Relational: Worries about people we love can keep us up at night. Before you go to bed spend some time praying for those you love who burden your heart and mind. Entrust them to God's care.

GUIDED JOURNALING

Right before bed tonight, take ten minutes to journal everything on your mind. Use this time to cast your cares on God, knowing that he cares for you.

WEEK 48
LOSING SLEEP OVER LOST SLEEP

> God hears us perfectly at all hours of the day. But . . . He's okay
> with calling you out of a comfortable sleep.
>
> *David R. Smith*

If after reading last week's entry you felt it did not describe your
exact struggle with sleep, you are not alone. Perhaps you can fall
asleep just fine but, like clockwork, you wake up at the same
time every night. Or maybe you are in a season of life, such as
parenting young children, where you are commonly awakened
in the middle of the night and can't go back to sleep. Perhaps you
work swing shifts and your body struggles to adjust to sleeping
at night. Dealing with patterns of insomnia is different than occasional difficulty with falling or staying asleep.

I (Eliza) can relate. I am a fragile sleeper. Once I am awakened, my mind can't seem to drift back to the land of nod. I used
to spend hours trying to fall asleep. My efforts to convince my
mind to go back to sleep were about as effective as convincing
oil and water to blend. Try as I might, eventually I ended up
right back where I started—wide awake. This reality would cause
stress and anxiety as the minutes turned into hours in the middle
of the night.

If this describes you as well, there is help. The Psalms give
us direction on how to use these waking spells. The wee hours
of the night can be spiritually productive when we use the time

to draw near to God rather than stress over lost sleep. Consider the following verses:

> By day the LORD commands his steadfast love, and at night his song is with me, a prayer to the God of my life. (Psalm 42:8)

> On my bed I remember you; I think of you through the watches of the night. (Psalm 63:6 NIV)

> At midnight I rise to praise you, because of your righteous rules. (Psalm 119:62)

> My eyes are awake before the watches of the night, that I may meditate on your promise. (Psalm 119:148)

One way to use the waking hours is to actually get out of bed and meditate on these verses. Get up and find a place to kneel and pray for all that is on your heart. Leave your bedroom, open God's Word, and read or work on a Bible study. When you become tired again, go back to bed and sleep.

Why get up? While there are spiritual benefits to drawing near to God in these wakeful hours, getting out of bed to do so is a way to attend to our bodies as we discussed in Week 13. Our bodies have a sleep cycle. This cycle, called the circadian rhythm, causes most sleep to happen at night. However, our sleep cycle can become disrupted, and we can end up waking up around the same time every night. There is also a mental connection that we subconsciously make that inhibits sleep when we lie awake in our beds for hours. On nights that you find yourself wide awake, getting up until the sleeplessness subsides prevents your mind from connecting your bed with wakefulness.

When we can't get back to sleep at night, we can try getting up to engage in rest-inducing activities outside of our beds. Activities like reading and writing promote mental wind-down and encourage sleep. This helps reset our sleep cycle.

Using sleepless nights to pray or meditate on the Word have been times of blessed engagement with the Lord for me. Not only do I have a lot less stress over lost sleep, but I also find God meets me in those times, more than if I had spent the hours trying to go back to sleep. Often, those nights are more valuable than if had I slept peacefully.

GOSPEL SPOTLIGHT

One of the most precious truths to meditate on is the fact that Jesus loves you and brought you into the family of God. You are God's precious and loved child. He cares for you and for the things you care about. Let that truth calm your midnight anxiety.

ACTION AND APPLICATION

Spiritual: The next time you are awake at night try getting up to spend time in prayer and reading the Scripture.

Emotional: Instead of stressing about the fact that you cannot sleep, trust that God can use these waking hours. Take your emotional concerns to the Lord by writing out a prayer to him.

Physical: When you find yourself awake at night, get up and do some stretches to relax any tense parts of your body. Find a comfortable place to do a body scan. Breathe through any painful tension you notice in your body.

Relational: Is someone you love causing your heart to be troubled in the middle of the night? Get out of bed and use the time to write them a note of encouragement. Let them know you are praying for them.

GUIDED JOURNALING

The next time you are awake at night consider the option of getting out of bed and journaling some of the thoughts, ideas, and prayers that are occupying your mind.

WEEK 49
THE ACCEPTED BROKEN
COMMANDMENT

> All God's commands are invitations to experience
> something better.
>
> *Mike Kelsey*

It has been said that the mechanic's car is the last one to get repaired and the plumber's faucet always leaks. This is not because they lack the skills to do the work. Rather, they are so busy fixing everybody else's problems that their own repairs have to wait. This same reality is often found among those in helping or serving vocations. Pastors, counselors, and other ministry workers tend to rarely pursue the care they faithfully give. You may find that you encourage others to get counseling, attend to their own needs, take a needed vacation, or schedule regular rest while neglecting those things yourself. If you are in the role of leader, mentor, caregiver, or teacher you also know exactly what I am talking about. What is it that makes the personal application of your own counsel so hard, specifically as it relates to the command to rest? One significant reason may surprise you.

Ministry is one vocation that inadvertently rewards overwork and overextending for the sake of others. An imbalanced application of the "one-anothers" in Scripture can eclipse simple obedience to God's command and invitation to rest (Exodus 20:8–10;

33:14; Leviticus 23:34; 1 Kings 8:56; Isaiah 57:2). But you don't have to be in full-time ministry to experience this. Those who regularly volunteer their time, work longer hours at their jobs, or continually give of themselves in a way that ignores their own needs tend to be applauded or praised as they carry out excessive demands. This is not to say we should run from opportunities to sacrificially serve others or work hard. Instead we should consider if these opportunities require us to neglect the command to rest.

Although Christian ministry can easily encourage avoiding rest, this would never be explicitly encouraged. In fact, you will hear the opposite. However, the certainty of unplanned meetings or calls requiring your attention and care involuntarily pull you back into serving. The demands of ministry do not respect the fact that you have already engaged in a full day of work. You can't schedule a crisis and you never know when suffering is going to come upon someone. No matter the timing, your job is to care and support. The more you show up for emergency needs, on top of managing normal responsibilities and tasks, the more you are seen as a faithful servant.

An undetected danger that comes with the acceptance of breaking the command to rest is that you become thought of as someone people can depend on or the star player. With this you can begin to feel validated and valuable. Fueled by vainglory, it's easy to keep the cycle of unrelenting work going. This is dangerous and can be symptomatic of misplaced worth and identity. Surrendering to a more balanced schedule that includes rest is actually more characteristic of a faithful servant of God than all the nonstop work you can do for others.

Although being "poured out as a drink offering" (Philippians 2:17) was modeled by Christ's ministers, it was not at the expense of neglecting God's invitation to rest (Psalm 116:7). You must be ready and willing to serve, but you also need to honor the command to keep the Sabbath (Exodus 23:12). As discussed in Week 45, God gave an entire day for rest and dependence on him. If you are in ministry or serve regularly at a church, you may have to choose a day other than Sunday to ensure you take the rest God commands.

Remember that setting aside time to rest provides an opportunity to intently worship and remember that God is in control. Taking time to rest allows you to proclaim that God is sovereign and able to take care of things while you recharge. God's commands are for your good. He never intended that service, ministry, or work be used as an excuse to break his commands. When we trust God enough to rest, we put our responsibilities in the place they belong—in the hands of our wise and sovereign God.

GOSPEL SPOTLIGHT

Jesus is the foremost model of a person who lived a life poured out in service while perfectly honoring God's invitation to rest. His faultless obedience to all of God's commands is why we can come freely to the Father even when we have failed in our own obedience.

ACTION AND APPLICATION

Spiritual: The Lord commands us and invites us to rest. How does rest regularly fit into your schedule?

Emotional: What emotions keep you overworking? Do you need to feel validated, worthy, valuable, or accomplished? The next time you overwork, stop and think about the emotions driving you.

Physical: What are some ways your body is telling you that you need to slow down and rest? Take a minute right now to do a Body Scan Activity found in the appendix and notice where you feel stress and tension.

Relational: Think of someone you work or serve with who can hold you accountable to regular rest. Reach out to that person today and talk with them about your plan to incorporate regular rest in your week. Set up a time to check in with them regularly.

GUIDED JOURNALING

This week's exercise requires you to take an honest look at what is driving your tendency to work without regular rest. Journal through each prompt carefully.

1. In what ways am I rewarded by overworking?
2. Who is the hardest person to say no to and why?

After completing these journal prompts ask God to help you make needed changes. Share this journal with the person keeping you accountable. Now finish this prayer:

Lord, thank you for your command and invitation to rest. I will rest this week and trust you with . . .

WEEK 50
SOLITUDE FOR SELF-CARE

As we walk through each day, responding to the needs of
those around us, we can become physically, emotionally, and
spiritually depleted. God has a never-ending supply of grace,
strength, and wisdom available that He wants to flow through
us to others. And we need to keep coming back into His
presence to get our supply replenished.

Nancy Leigh DeMoss

How do you feel about being alone? For some, time spent alone
sounds like a glorious reprieve. For others, it elicits negative feelings ranging from mild discomfort to absolute terror. We all need
both solitude and community to flourish, and our relational tendencies toward introversion or extroversion impact which of these
needs feels more natural.

No matter your personal tendency, solitude is an important
means of self-care that we find modeled in the life of Jesus. Regardless of how busy he became, Jesus was unapologetic in the
practice of stepping away. He did not wait for things to slow
down. As we discussed in Week 2, he stepped away to be alone
even in his busiest seasons of ministry.

What about you? When was the last time you were alone?
Even people who desire solitude often find it difficult to step
away. Life is easily scheduled to the brim. Even when we do step
away from people, solitude has become more elusive because

of technology. We aren't truly alone when we are checking our email, receiving social media notifications, and responding to every text that comes to our phone. True solitude requires us to step away from people *and* our devices.

This is an uncomfortable thought for many. What if we are needed? What if problems arise that only we can solve? Making ourselves unavailable can feel unrealistic or selfish. If someone needs something, isn't that more important than indulging in a personal desire or need for space? In Luke 4, Jesus answers this question in an unexpected way. Crowds of people come to him at sunset, and he heals many of them. Jesus presumably works all night, and finally at daybreak, he leaves to find a moment of solitude before moving on to other towns. Even though people are searching for him—likely many of them sick and in need of healing—he still chooses to disappear into the wilderness.

On this occasion, Jesus put his need for time alone before the needs of the crowds who followed him. Jesus could have healed more sick people if he had not taken this time away. Why did he do this? While solitude has many benefits, Jesus's main reason for stepping away throughout his ministry was to spend time with God. Jesus drew his strength from his Father. He depended on God and never attempted to do anything without him (John 5:19).

Times of solitude provide the ideal context for us to meet with God. Have you been seeking time out with God since we first discussed this in Week 2? Skipping this time can feel tempting. It's easy to be drawn into people's needs from the moment we wake up to the minute we fall asleep. But like Jesus, we should not attempt to meet other people's needs to the neglect of our own need for God.

Solitude provides a setting for us to depend on God and draw strength from him through times of prayer, Scripture reading, and other spiritual disciplines. As he meets our needs for physical and spiritual rest, we are fueled to then meet the needs of others. If Jesus needed solitude, how much more do we?

GOSPEL SPOTLIGHT

Time alone with God is a foretaste of eternity when we will be with him forever. Jesus has secured for us a lasting relationship with God that we can begin to experience even now.

ACTION AND APPLICATION

Spiritual: How could times of solitude provide a context for you to prioritize your relationship with God and connect with him through spiritual practices?

Emotional: Times of solitude provide the opportunity to notice emotions that are harder to identify when we are distracted with tasks and people. Take some time to be alone. Ask yourself this question: what are your emotions revealing about your need to spend time alone with God?

Physical: Identify a place where you can be alone. What electronic devices or other distractions do you need to physically separate yourself from to truly be alone?

Relational: Do you consider yourself to be an introvert or an extrovert? How does your answer impact your desire for solitude?

GUIDED JOURNALING

The following prompts can help you explore what impedes times of solitude.

God, the distractions that pull me away from solitude with you are . . .

Help me to surrender these concerns to you, so I can be more fully in your presence. I need _____ from you, so I can better serve you.

WEEK 51
SELF-CARE IS NOT A SAVIOR

God graciously lets us wear ourselves out. Life exists not in us
but in Christ alone and Christ fully.

Ray Ortlund

Finding freedom to prioritize self-care can be life-changing for
some people. We hope this has been the case for you. We also
realize it's possible you still feel stuck. As I (Esther) finished writing this book, I was convicted that some of our suggestions may
feel a bit discouraging. It's possible you have followed through
on our suggestions and yet felt your efforts didn't work. No matter how hard you try and no matter how many changes you
make, you are still drowning in the circumstances of your life.

If this has been your experience, I can relate. I can think of
long periods of time in my life when I practiced self-care strategies and still felt burned out. Nothing seemed to help. Despite
going to the doctor, my body stayed broken. I gave what little
energy I had to my relationships, but it wasn't enough for them
to flourish. No amount of journaling, deep breathing, rest, asking
for help, or eating healthy could cure my sadness. My relationship
with God centered on cries for help, and while this was appropriate for the circumstances, I wanted to feel joy in his presence.

Rest and self-care do not always prevent burnout. Sometimes burnout is a form of suffering that comes from the circumstances of living in a broken world. No matter how faithfully

we care for ourselves, we may not be able to experience whole-life thriving. It's difficult to grapple with the reality that some burnout has no earthly solution. If this describes you, I want to encourage you that even this realization has purpose.

Thinking back on seasons when self-care offered me little help or solace, I can see now that God was gently redirecting me toward himself. These seasons reminded me that what I need most is Jesus. A relaxing bubble bath may soothe physical aches for a moment, but only Jesus can soothe the soul. A good movie can warm the heart for an hour or two but only Jesus can sustain us through the storms of life. Self-care is not a savior. No strategy of this world is sufficient to save our wandering hearts.

In 1 Corinthians 15:3, Paul tells us what we should consider to be "of first importance." He reminds us of the gospel that saves: "that Christ died for our sins according to the Scriptures, that he was buried, that he was raised on the third day according to the Scriptures" (1 Corinthians 15:3–4 NIV). God often uses times when we feel weak and helpless to remind us of the good news that should be of first importance in our lives. When our self-care strategies fall short and we realize that we cannot save ourselves, we are drawn to more fully rely on Christ.

I don't regret taking time to care for myself in those seasons when self-care felt futile. My efforts honored God, and my heart, mind, body, and relationships would have been far worse off if I had done nothing. But these self-care efforts were secondary to what I needed most. God revealed what was most important. It was my relationship with Christ—a relationship that was sufficient in moments when self-care was not.

GOSPEL SPOTLIGHT

Colossians 2:10 says that you have been "made complete" (NIV) or "brought to fullness" (NASB) through your union with Christ. Though you may feel broken, Christ has made you perfect

(Hebrews 10:4). He is sufficient to meet each and every one of your spiritual needs.

ACTION AND APPLICATION

Spiritual: Do you find yourself relying on your self-care efforts when you should be relying on Christ? Read Philippians 4:19. Meditate on the sufficiency of Christ to meet your needs.

Emotional: The psalmist writes, "My flesh and my heart may fail, but God is the strength of my heart and my portion forever" (Psalm 73:26). Memorize this passage and draw it to mind when emotional struggles feel overwhelming.

Physical: Paul writes, "For the sake of Christ, then, I am content with weaknesses, insults, hardships, persecutions, and calamities. For when I am weak, then I am strong" (2 Corinthians 12:10). Pray for Christ to show you his strength in your weakness.

Relational: People may fail us or abandon us, but God is an ever-present source of help and comfort (Psalm 46:1). How can this truth comfort you today?

GUIDED JOURNALING

Journal through some of the ways God has shown up for you. How has he shown himself to be faithful in times when self-care efforts weren't enough?

WEEK 52
FOREVER AT REST

[Jesus said,] "Take my yoke upon you and learn from me, for I am gentle and humble in heart, and you will find rest for your souls."

Matthew 11:29 NIV

Rest is not only for our mortal lives on earth. God's plan is for rest to be a part of our lives for eternity. When we think about all that we will do in heaven, worship dominates the description. Another common theme found in Scripture about heaven is often forgotten: the invitation to rest.

In heaven we will rest from our labors (Revelation 14:13), but rest is not just something we will do. Rest will be our state. It will be our location. We *enter it* forever (Hebrews 4:9–12). In the presence of Jesus, face-to-face, we will fully experience what it means to rest. Entering into the fullness of our glorification in heaven, we will realize fully the work Jesus accomplished. We will be finally without sin. This is rest. To live untainted by remaining sin means all we do will be exactly right. We will never again have the regret that comes from doing something we shouldn't have or not doing something we should have. What peace, what rest!

This rest is only possible because of the finished work of Jesus. Jesus purchased this eternal rest for us with his blood. Apart from Jesus, we cannot come to God. We enter this rest because of his atoning sacrifice. Jesus made a way for us to enter into eternal rest with the Lord, but entering into this rest is a choice each of us must make (Romans 10:9).

To enter this rest, you must put your trust in the work of Jesus alone (John 14:6). You will never be able to do enough to earn your way to heaven. You can't work hard enough to deserve God's favor. The only way to eternal rest is to rest right now in the work of Jesus. So in this final week, if you have not trusted in the work Jesus did when he died in your place and paid for your sins, now is the time. If you have questions about this, talk to a Christian friend or pastor or read one of the Gospels to learn directly from the life of Jesus.

If you have already trusted in Jesus, let this reminder encourage you that you do not have to work to prove anything to God or earn your standing with him. You can rest in the work of Jesus now as you wait for the fullness of God's rest in heaven. Let this good news encourage you on the most overwhelming days. On days when it feels like the demands of your life are insurmountable, remember that the most needed work is already done in Jesus. God's plan includes rest now, and rest encompasses our future.

As we end our journey together, consider what brings you rest in life. A completed to-do list? A clean house? A deadline met? An assignment turned in on time? Assurance that you and your family are safe and healthy? The ability to take that needed vacation? As believers our rest is not dependent on things like these. We rest, both now and forever, in the work Jesus accomplished on our behalf.

GOSPEL SPOTLIGHT

"They will rest from their labor, for their deeds will follow them" (Revelation 14:13 NIV). "This is my resting place forever; here I will dwell, for I have desired it" (Psalm 132:14).

ACTION AND APPLICATION

Spiritual: Are you resting in the work of Jesus? Take some time to remember all Jesus has done. Consider reading through the Gospels over the next couple months as a way to remind your heart of this reality.

Emotional: Jesus promises eternal rest in heaven. As you imagine this promise fulfilled, what thoughts and feelings arise? Write them down.

Physical: Read Ephesians 2:8–9. Resting our souls in Jesus can promote physical rest, because when we know we are right with God, we don't overwork to prove ourselves. Take time to rest your body this week in the knowledge that you are saved by grace through faith, not through your works.

Relational: Who in your life needs to hear the message of the rest that is available in Jesus? Take a moment to text them now and ask if you can meet up to chat. Pray for an opportunity to share about the rest that is found in Jesus.

GUIDED JOURNALING

For this final journaling exercise, take your time finishing this sentence: Jesus, thank you for making a way for me to be forever at rest. I praise you for . . .

CONCLUSION

As we close this journey, we hope you have been encouraged to embrace the concept that caring for yourself is an important practice for all believers. You may have found some weeks refreshing while other weeks posed major challenges. If you have found it difficult to maintain a balanced life, you are not alone. There isn't a single lesson in this book that we haven't needed to apply and reapply to our own lives. Whole-life stewardship is hard. Really hard!

We have prayed for you throughout the process of writing this book. We've prayed that you would understand God's love and concern for your personal well-being. We've prayed for you to embrace the value of caring for yourself so you can better care for others. It is our prayer that you will flourish as you implement biblical principles of self-care into your whole life.

As you practiced self-care this year, what did you find that *you* most need from God? We each have self-care needs that differ depending on our personalities, strengths, weaknesses, and current season of life. Certain practices will be more important to one person than to another. As you think back on the strategies that were offered in this book, which do you find most helpful? Which practices are most necessary to your ability to care for yourself and others?

These are important questions to consider because it is easy to slip out of self-care practices. Even as we wrote this book, we were reminded of how tempting it can be to skip attending to our own needs to work on just one more page of writing. We are still learning how to faithfully practice what it means to steward our whole lives in a balanced, God-glorifying way. As we write these final words, in many ways it feels like only the beginning. Now the hard work comes—applying them!

Your journey doesn't end here either. To sustain self-care throughout your life requires lifelong attention. In light of that, we have one final action and application. We recommend that you revisit the concepts in this book until they become ingrained into your regular routine. The best way to accomplish that is to plan to go back through this book again. If you completed this book on your own, consider reading it with a friend or a group of people. Is there someone you know who would benefit from the practices in this book? Does your small group, ministry team, book club, fellow classmate, or business colleague need a self-care makeover? If, on the other hand, you went through this book with others, now go back and do it on your own. We have no doubt you will gain from that process. This may be the end of the book, but don't let it be the end of the journey. Keep practicing rhythms of self-care until they become infused into your whole life.

And finally, for all of our readers, we pray these words: "Now to him who is able to do far more abundantly than all that we ask or think, according to the power at work within us, to him be glory in the church and in Christ Jesus throughout all generations, forever and ever. Amen" (Ephesians 3:20–21).

Keep it going. Join others in engaging in whole-life stewardship. To further connect with the content and authors be sure to follow @WholeLifeBook on Facebook, Twitter, and Instagram.

APPENDIX

BULLET JOURNALING

Journaling is a helpful tool to process thoughts, but not everyone is a journaler. A bullet journal can be a great alternative to the more traditional way of writing out your thoughts. The bullet journal method was developed by author Ryder Carroll as an organizational tool to harness mindfulness and productivity into intentionality. He states that, "Bullet Journaling acts as a bridge between your beliefs and your actions."[13] His method is designed to help people "learn how to stop reacting and start responding."[14]

A bullet journal is exactly what the name describes. Instead of journaling out your thoughts and feelings in complete sentences and paragraphs, a bullet journal allows you to capture the gist of things in just a few words. Don't worry about grammar or punctuation. The key is to get your thoughts out on a page. Bullet journaling is also known as BuJo. Just like the abbreviated nickname, bullet journaling is an abbreviated approach to journaling. We suggest an adaptation of Carroll's method as a means to help you process your struggles and remember important truths.

Setup

Use a small notebook or create a note on your phone or computer. Label it "BuJo" to easily identify it as your bullet journal.

Journaling

On a clean page title your journal entry (e.g., Prayers, Promises, To-Do, or whatever fits your need). Next, begin to write the thoughts connected to the entry title in short phrases or single words. Mark each thought with a bullet as you go.

Example

God's Faithfulness to Me

- Provided a job
- Friendship with John and Jane
- Health
- School
- Healing in family
- Church family
- Safe place to live

Once you're done, notice how writing these things down made you feel. Keep the bullet journal and review it often. Make new journal entries as needed.

BREATHING EXERCISES

Most people are unaware of their breathing until something noticeably alters it. Run up a flight of stairs and you will be aware of a change in your breathing. Lay down on the couch for ten minutes and you may become aware your breathing has slowed. In reality our breathing changes far more often than we notice. Stress, anxiety, and a busy mind can change our breathing. This can trigger the body to remain in high alert and increase anxiety.

Breathing exercises offer a simple and effective way to regulate your breath and reverse the stress reaction in your body. Breathing exercises should be a regular part of your day. Much like good nutrition, exercise, and sleep, attention to your breathing is very important to promote a healthier lifestyle and reduce stress, and it only takes a few minutes!

Here are a few breathing exercises to try. Read the instructions, then practice the exercise.

Simple Breathing Exercise

1. Wherever you are, take a minute to notice your body. Get as comfortable as possible. If you are able, close your eyes.
2. Slowly take a deep, controlled breath in through your nose or mouth.
3. Exhale slowly and relax your body as you do so.
4. Repeat two to three times.

Deep Breathing Exercise (Four, Seven, Eight, Four Breathing)

1. Sit or lay comfortably in a place where you will be undisturbed.
2. Close your eyes and focus on your normal breath.
3. Empty your lungs of air.
4. Take a deep breath in for four counts. Do not tense your shoulders or neck.
5. Hold the breath for seven counts.
6. Slowly exhale for eight counts, relaxing your body as you do.
7. Once you are done exhaling, count to four.
8. Repeat two to three times.

Deep Breathing Exercise with Scripture

Using the deep breathing technique described above, use a line of Scripture instead of the counting as you inhale and exhale. Example:

Breathe in while saying in your mind, *Cast your cares on him.*

Breathe out while saying in your mind, *Because he cares for you.*

Alternatively, you can listen to Scripture read aloud from an app or online as you practice breathing deeply, instead of meditating on a line of Scripture in your mind.

BODY SCAN

The Body Scan Activity is a way to become more aware of how your body may be holding or experiencing tension, discomfort, aches, pain, or stress. Focused attention on your body allows you to intentionally relax and release tight muscles. It also increases your awareness of how your body responds to various life circumstances.

The best way to do a body scan is to ask someone to read the script to you. If you are working through this book with a friend or a group, ask someone to slowly read the script out loud. If you are doing this exercise alone, consider recording yourself reading the script. Another option is to read through the script completely to familiarize yourself with the activity before attempting to put it into practice.

Body Scan Script

1. Find a quiet room and make yourself comfortable. You may choose to sit down, or you may lie on your back. Let your hands rest in your lap or at your side.
2. If you feel comfortable, close your eyes. Or if you prefer, look softly in one direction instead. Begin by taking several long, slow, deep breaths, breathing in through your nose and out through your mouth. Feel your stomach and rib cage expand as you inhale. Allow your body to relax as you exhale. (Reader pause.)
3. If you can hear noises or sounds around you, mentally set them aside. Shift your attention from what is happening outside your body to what is happening inside your body.

4. (Reader pause.) Anytime you get distracted by sounds or thoughts around you, simply notice this and bring your focus back to your body and your breathing.

5. Starting at your feet, notice what you feel. What physical sensations do you notice? If you don't feel anything, that is okay too. Just notice that. (Reader pause.) Wiggle your toes. Roll your ankles. Notice how they feel. Are you wearing shoes or socks? Notice how they feel on your feet. Are they tight? Soft? Warm? Sweaty? If you are barefoot, simply take note of how your feet feel. Take a deep breath in and think about sending that breath all the way to your toes. (Reader pause.)

6. Now move your attention from your feet up to your ankles (reader pause) and then to your calves. Take another deep breath and relax your muscles in your ankles and calves. Make whatever adjustments your body needs to be comfortable. (Reader pause.)

7. When you are ready, breathe into the rest of your legs and notice how your muscles feel. Pay attention to your hamstrings and thighs. Soften any tension that you feel. (Reader pause.) Has your mind started to wander? If so, bring your attention back to your body and take a deep breath. Stay focused on your legs a little longer, paying attention to what you feel.

8. On your next inhale, move your attention to your pelvis and lower back. Exhale and relax this area, paying attention to any discomfort as you breathe. If you need to take another breath to release the tension, do so slowly. (Reader pause.)

9. Moving on from your lower back, notice your abdomen and chest. Is any tension or anxiety present as you focus on this area? (Reader pause.) Take a deep breath and send the oxygen to your gut, filling it completely. Exhale slowly and observe any release of negative sensations. Notice how

your clothes feel on this part of your body. Where can
you feel them on your belly and chest? How do they feel
against your skin? Notice it and breathe. (Reader pause.)

10. Gently wiggle your arms. As you do, soften the muscles
in your upper and lower arms. As you breathe, let them
rest softly in one place. Now pay attention to your fingers.
Can you mentally soften each one of your fingers from
your pinkies to your thumbs? (Reader pause.)

11. Now notice your upper back and shoulders. Is there any
pain, tightness, stiffness, or aches? Without any judgment, pay attention to areas of discomfort and make
any needed adjustments to help release the tension. Take
a deep breath in, and as you slowly exhale, soften your
shoulders. Let go of any tension. Notice any changes or
shifts. (Reader pause.)

12. Move from your shoulders to your neck and scalp. With
the same focus, notice any tense muscles. Breathe deeply,
relaxing any tension you feel. The muscles in your scalp
should relax from the top of your head to the base of your
neck. (Reader pause.)

13. Next move to your face. Soften your face and imagine
your facial muscles are soft, warm clay. Breathe in slowly,
and as you exhale, let those muscles simply rest on the
bones in your face, dissolving any tension. (Reader pause.)

14. Take a few slow deep breaths, noticing your entire body.
Feel your whole body relax into the chair or floor.

15. As you finish, shift your focus back to where you are in
the present moment. Open your eyes. Recognize how
much care and time you gave to your body.

ACKNOWLEDGMENTS

We cannot express how thrilled we are to know that a book like this now exists. It was our privilege to create a resource that not only enriches our lives but also the lives of others. But this would have never happened on our own.

Together we want to thank the team at New Growth Press who also believed this book was needed. The edits and suggestions offered by Barbara and Ruth helped us give this book a richer application. We also want to thank friends who were willing to brainstorm the concept and title, read early manuscripts, and offer commendations when it was only an idea and an outline. John, Jeremy, Alison, Carol, Marian, Jonathan, and Tim, your input helped more than you know.

Personally I (Eliza) want to thank Esther. I am quite sure there isn't anyone I would have rather written this book with. You prayerfully invested hours of focused care and agonizing effort in preparing this little project for the real world. Who knew writing a book would feel so much like co-parenting? Your perspective brought balance, and this book would be inferior without you.

I also want to thank my amazing family who are a continual reminder of why it is so important to care for myself. They are also my biggest fans, and their excitement for this book has been an encouragement beyond words. Ken, Aaron, Ashton, Annalisa, and Adam, you are a source of joy and refreshment to my soul.

I (Esther) want to thank Eliza. You are an unending source of brilliant ideas, and the concept behind this book ranks up there as one of your best. I am so grateful that you invited me to join you in creating this important resource. I couldn't have asked for a better coauthoring experience! Your tireless work and spot-on feedback made this book the best it could be.

Thank you also to my husband, Ian, who reminds me to take breaks, asks me if I ate lunch, questions why I am working on the weekend, and supports every writing project I have ever taken on. I am more hydrated and less caffeinated because of you.

ENDNOTES

1. Mark Good, *Real Talk: Creating Space for Hearts to Change* (Sisters, Oregon: Deep River Books, 2017), 39–50.

2. Mark Vroegop, *Dark Clouds, Deep Mercy: Discovering the Grace of Lament* (Wheaton, Illinois: Crossway, 2019).

3. June Bell, "Fitting in Exercise on Company Time and the Company's Dime," *Society for Human Resource Management*, May 23, 2017, https://www.shrm.org/resourcesandtools/legal-and-compliance/state-and-local-updates/pages/fitting-in-fitness-on-company-time.aspx/.

4. Elisa Silverman, "How Leadership Can Reap Big Rewards By Creating A 'Self-Care Culture'," *15Five Blog*, retrieved August 31, 2020, https://www.15five.com/blog/work-culture-self-care/.

5. Jennifer M. Taber, Bryan Leyva, and Alexander Persoskie, "Why Do People Avoid Medical Care? A Qualitative Study Using National Data," *Journal of General Internal Medicine* 30, no. 3 (March 2015): 290–297, https://doi.org/10.1007/s11606-014-3089-1.

6. Charles Hodges, "Medication: Right or Wrong? Wise or Unwise? Helpful or Not?" *Biblical Counseling Coalition,* August 24, 2018, https://www.biblicalcounselingcoalition.org/2018/08/24/medication-right-or-wrong-wise-or-unwise-helpful-or-not/.

7. J. Alasdair Groves and Winston T. Smith, *Untangling Emotions: God's Gift of Emotions* (Wheaton, Illinois: Crossway, 2019), 93–101.

8. Maria Godoy, "New World Health Organization Data Confirms Around 80% Of Cases Are Mild," NPR, February 17, 2020, https://www.npr.org/2020/02/17/806729340/new-world-health-organization-data-confirms-around-80-of-cases-are-mild/.

9. George T. Doran, "There's a S.M.A.R.T. Way to Write Management's Goals and Objectives," *Management Review* 70, no. 11 (1981): 35–36.

10. Blue Letter Bible, "katamanthanō," lexicon:: Strong's G2648, https://www.blueletterbible.org/lang/lexicon/lexicon.cfm?Strongs=G2648&t=ESV.

11. Dane Calvin Ortlund, *Gentle and Lowly: The Heart of Christ for Sinners and Sufferers* (Wheaton, Illinois: Crossway, 2020), 99.

12. Carey Nieuwhof, "Rest, Celebration and God," *Carey Niewohof* blog, https://careynieuwhof.com/rest-celebratio/.

13. Ryder Carroll, *The Bullet Journal Method: Track the Past, Order the Present, Design the Future* (New York, New York: Portfolio, 2018), 18.

14. Carroll, *The Bullet Journal Method*, 20.